JOHN LANCHESTER

The Wall

Cornelsen

John Lanchester **The Wall**

Annotationen und Zusatzmaterialien: Dr. Peter Hohwiller
Verlagsredaktion: Elke Lehmann (Redaktionsleitung), Dr. Jan Dreßler
Umschlagkonzept: Cornelsen Verlag GmbH
Umschlaggestaltung: Klein & Halm Grafikdesign
Umschlagfoto: Shutterstock.com/Pim Kraster
Layout und technische Umsetzung: L101 Mediengestaltung, Fürstenwalde

www.cornelsen.de

1. Auflage, 3. Druck 2023

This edition is the complete and unabridged text of the novel.

Alle Drucke dieser Auflage sind inhaltlich unverändert und
können im Unterricht nebeneinander verwendet werden.

Druck: AZ Druck und Datentechnik GmbH, Kempten

ISBN 978-3-06-035955-4

PEFC
PEFC/04-31-2260

PEFC-zertifiziert
Dieses Produkt
stammt aus
nachhaltig
bewirtschafteten
Wäldern und
kontrollierten Quellen
www.pefc.de

Contents

In memory of Peggie Geraghty

Abbreviations and Annotations

adj	adjective	n	noun
AE	American English	pl	plural
BE	British English	sb.	somebody
derog	derogatory	sl	slang
e.g.	exempli gratia; for example	sth.	something
i.e.	id est, that is	usu.	usually
fml	formal	v	verb
infml	informal		

The annotations are arranged chronologically; the first time a word is used is where you will find it explained.

I

THE WALL

1

It's cold on the Wall. That's the first thing everybody tells you, and the first thing you notice when you're sent there, and it's the thing you think about all the time you're on it, and it's the thing you remember when you're not there any more. It's cold on the Wall.

You look for metaphors. It's cold as slate[1], as diamond, as the moon. Cold as charity[2] – that's a good one. But you soon realise that the thing about the cold is that it isn't a metaphor. It isn't like anything else. It's nothing but a physical fact. This kind of cold, anyway. Cold is cold is cold.

So that's the first thing that hits you. It isn't like other cold. This is a cold that is all about the place, like a permanent physical attribute of the location. The cold is one of its fundamental properties[3]; it's intrinsic[4]. So it hits you as a package, the first time you go to the Wall, on the first day of your tour. You know that you are there for two years. You know that it's basically the same everywhere, as far as the geography goes, but that everything depends on what the people you will be serving with are like. You know that there's nothing you can do about that. It is frightening but also in its way a little bit freeing. No choice – everything about the Wall means you have no choice.

You get a little training but not much. Six weeks. Mainly it's about how to hold, clean, look after and fire your weapon. In that order. Some fitness training, but not much; a lot of training in midnight awakening, sleep disruption[5], sudden panics, sudden changes of order, small-hours[6] tests of discipline. They drum[7] that into you: dis-

1 slate: dark grey stone **2** charity: compassion for other people **3** property: quality, feature **4** intrinsic: belonging to sth. **5** disruption: *Unterbrechung* **6** small-hours: early hours of the day **7** drum sth. into sb.: say sth. to sb. again and again so that it is remembered

cipline trumps[1] courage. In a fight, the people who win are the ones who do what they're told. It's not like it is in films. Don't be brave, just do what you're told. That's pretty much it. The rest of the training happens on the Wall. You get it from the Defenders who've been there longer than you. Then in your turn you give it to the Defenders who come after. So that's what you arrive able to do: get up in the middle of the night, and look after your weapon.

You usually arrive after dark. I don't know why but that's just how they do it. Already you had a long day to get there: walk, bus, train, second train, lorry[2]. The lorry drops you off. You and your rucksack are left standing there in the cold and the blackness. There is the Wall in front of you, a long low concrete[3] monster. It stretches into the distance. Although the Wall is completely vertical, when you stand underneath it, it feels as if it overhangs. As if it could topple[4] over onto you. You feel leant on.

The air is full of moisture, even when it isn't actually wet, which it often is, either with rain or with sea-spray splashing over the top. It isn't usually windy, immediately behind the Wall, but it sometimes is. In the dark and the damp[5], the Wall looks black. The only path or sign or hint for what you should do or where you should go is a flight of concrete steps – they always drop you near the steps. There's a small light at the top, in the guard house, but you don't yet know that's what you're looking at. Instead what you mainly think is that the Wall is taller than you expected. Of course you've seen it before, in real life, and in pictures, maybe even in your dreams. (That's one of the things you learn on the Wall: that lots of people dream about it, long before they're sent there.) But when you're standing at the bottom looking up, and you know you're going to be there for two years, and that the best thing that can happen to you in those two years is that you survive and get off the Wall and never have to spend another day of your life anywhere near it – then it looks different. It looks very tall and very straight and very dark.

1 trump sth.: be better than sth. **2** lorry (BE): truck (AE) **3** concrete (n): *Beton*
4 topple over onto sb./sth.: fall on sb./sth. **5** damp (n): moisture, humidity

(It is.) The exposed concrete stairs look steep and slippery. (They are.) It looks like a cold, hard, unforgiving, desperate place. (It is.) You feel trapped. (You are.) You are longing for this to be over; longing to be somewhere else; you would give anything not to be here. Maybe, even if you're not religious, you say a prayer, out loud or under your breath, it doesn't matter, because it doesn't change anything, because your prayer says, please please please let me get off the Wall, and yet there you are, on the Wall. You start up the steps. You've begun your life on the Wall.

I was shaking as I went up the stairs; I'd like to think it was from the cold but it was probably half that and half fear. There was no guard rail[1] and the concrete was more and more damp as I climbed. I've never been good with heights, even quite low ones. It crossed my mind that I might slip and fall off and that thought grew as I got higher up. I'm going to fall off and split my head open and die, and my time on the Wall will be over before it's even begun, I thought. I'll be a punchline[2]. Remember that idiot who ...? But if that happens, at least I'll be off the Wall.

At the top I got to the guard house. Light was coming through a frosted[3] window. I couldn't see in. I didn't know where to go or what to do, but there were no other options, so I knocked. There was no reply. I knocked again and heard a noise and took that as a sign to go in.

I stepped in and a wave of warmth flooded over me. My glasses immediately fogged up so I couldn't see. I heard somebody laugh and somebody else say something under their breath. I took my glasses off and squinted[4] around. The room was an undecorated concrete box. The walls were covered in maps. Two people sat in the opposite corners, one of them an imposing[5] black man with scarred cheeks wearing an olive-green cabled[6] uniform sweater. This was the Captain, though I didn't know that yet. He was the only person

1 guard rail: *Geländer* **2** punchline: last and funny line of a joke **3** frosted (glass): *Milchglas* **4** squint (v): look at sth. with your eyes half shut **5** imposing: impressive **6** cabled: *mit einem Zopfmuster versehen*

on the Wall I ever saw wearing uniform. For the rest of us it simply wasn't warm enough. He looked at me unsmiling. Behind him there were three computer monitors with a green-screen radar display.

'A Defender who can't see,' he said. 'Great.'

The other person snorted[1]. This was a heavy-set white man wearing a red knitted cap: the Sergeant, though I didn't know that yet either.

'I'm Kavanagh,' I eventually said. 'I'm new.' It seems idiotic now and it seemed idiotic then, but I had no idea what else to say. The two of them didn't even laugh. They just looked at me. The man in uniform got up and walked over to me and looked me up and down. He was tall, at least half a head taller than me.

'I'm the Captain,' he said. 'This is the Sergeant. Do everything we tell you to without questioning why. It takes about four months before you know what you're doing. I have complete power to extend your stay here, without appeal[2]. I don't have to give a reason. The only way you get off the Wall is that two years go past, and I decide to let you go. If they didn't make that clear in training, I'm making it clear now. Is it clear?' It was. I said so.

'Take him to the barracks[3],' he said to the Sergeant. 'I'm going out on the Wall.'

He left. The Sergeant's demeanour changed a little when he was on his own.

'Right,' he said. 'There are two sergeants, one for each shift. I'm yours. The other one is on the Wall. I should be in bed but I stayed up to meet you because I'm a fucking saint. Ask anyone. You'll meet the rest of your shift in the morning. I'll give you a quick version of the tour. The rest you can fill in tomorrow. Like the Captain said, it takes a while for it all to sink in[4], and the best way is through repetition. You can ask questions at the beginning but everyone gets sick

1 snort: make a sound by breathing through your nose to express amusement at sb./sth. **2** appeal: formal request to take back a decision **3** barracks (pl): houses for soldiers **4** sink in: be fully understood

of that pretty quickly, so I'd advise you to think if there's an obvious answer to whatever it is you're asking before you open your gob[1].'

He showed me around the mess hall[2], which was a bare concrete box with tables and chairs, the rec room[3], which was a bare concrete box with a huge television and badly battered[4] sofas, the armoury[5], which was locked, and the infirmary[6], which was a bare concrete box with four steel-framed beds and no medical staff. Then he led me down two flights of stairs to the barracks, which is what Defenders called the room where everyone slept. It too was a bare concrete box. After standing in the entrance for about a minute, my eyes adapted enough to be able to make out the main details. There were thirty beds in the room, fifteen on each side, with plywood partitions[7] separating them into cubicles[8]. At the far end was the washroom. I was already familiar with the layout, because it was the same as in the barracks where I had done my training. One side had no external light source, the other had small square windows above head height. The beds along the right-hand wall were all empty, because that half of the company was on night duty. The beds along the left-hand wall were all occupied by sleeping bodies, except the ninth bed along, which had been empty and was now mine.

I put my bag down in the back of the cubicle. I took off my shoes and my outer layers of clothing and got into the bed. The sheets were rough but the two blankets were thick and I quickly warmed up. I could hear snores and muttering[9] from my new squad[10] companions. Being hungry makes me speedy[11]; I realised I hadn't eaten since setting out[12], and that my mind was whirring[13] too fast to sleep. Tired, wakeful, apprehensive[14], I lay there and looked at the ceiling,

1 gob (sl): mouth **2** mess hall: room where soldiers eat **3** rec room (infml): recreation room: room where soldiers spend their free time **4** battered: old and very used **5** armoury: place where weapons are kept **6** infirmary: medical rooms **7** plywood partition: *Trennwand aus Sperrholz* **8** cubicle: small room made by dividing a larger room **9** mutter: speak unintelligibly in a low voice **10** squad: small group of soldiers **11** speedy: fast, (here) agitated **12** set out: leave **13** whir (v): (here) spin, be agitated **14** apprehensive: worried, frightened

and thought, I only have two years of this, 729 more nights, after I get through this one. That's if I'm lucky and nothing goes wrong.

I must have slept, because I was woken up. Or maybe it was a new kind of sleep where you have none of the good part of being asleep but all of the bad part of being jolted awake[1]. I heard an alarm and a few moments later felt the bed shake and opened my eyes to see a man's face leaning down over me, close enough to smell his hot, faintly rank[2] breath. The face was all beard, eyes and wool cap. On the upside, he was smiling.

'New meat,' he said. 'I'm the Corporal. Also known as Yos. Five minutes to wash, fifteen to breakfast, then we assemble.' He shook the bed one more time, as if for luck, then stood up and headed towards the washroom. He was another tall man, well over six feet[3]. Around him other squad members were getting up, grumbling[4] and scratching. I saw that most of them slept more or less fully clothed. The Corporal stopped a few metres away and turned to me.

'Don't look so worried,' he said. 'You know that thing they say, don't worry, it might never happen? This is different. You're on the Wall. It already has.' He laughed and left me.

Thirty in a company, divided into two squads or shifts of fifteen. In addition, five-odd[5] permanent staff at each guard station, cooks and cleaners. Companies rotate, two weeks on the Wall, two weeks off. One of those weeks is training and general maintenance[6] and whatever, the other is leave[7]. Squads only change members when people have finished their time on the Wall. That's a rolling process, so there are always Defenders who are coming up to the end of their time, mixed in with others who've just started. Those are the two

1 jolt sb./sth.: shake sb./sth. **2** rank (adj): with a strong unpleasant smell
3 1 foot = 30.48 cm **4** grumble: complain **5** five-odd: five or a little more
6 maintenance: all work necessary for keeping sth. in good condition **7** leave (n): permitted absence from service

twitchiest[1] groups, the ones who've only just begun and haven't got a clue what they're doing, and the ones at the end who feel they can reach out with their tongues and taste the freedom of life after the Wall, and who can think of only two subjects, how great it will be to get away and what a disaster it would be if anything went wrong in the last few days. The Defenders in the middle, some distance from both the beginning and the end, are more stoic.

In my squad I'd already met the Sergeant and the Corporal: they were always easy to tell apart, at whatever distance and however thickly swaddled[2] in cold-weather clothing, because the Sergeant was heavy and the Corporal was tall. We called the Sergeant Sarge and we called the Corporal Yos. His hobby was whittling[3], and when we weren't on the Wall he was usually working on a piece of wood with a wicked-looking curved knife. As for the other members of the squad, that first morning and for several days to come, telling people apart was an issue. It was the layers. So many layers! At breakfast, their heads down over porridge, silent, my new companions were difficult to distinguish even by gender. Everybody goes to the Wall and the balance overall is fifty–fifty, so by probability half of my squad should be women, but there was basically no way of knowing who was who except by asking, and it didn't seem an ideal icebreaker.

After breakfast we went to the wardroom[4] for a briefing[5] from the Captain. The battered, unloved desks and chairs made it look like a school. There were two maps behind him, one a detailed 3D projection of our section of Wall and the other at a smaller scale[6] showing the nearest fifty kilometres of coast. I was to learn that the briefing almost always had no relevant news, other than the temperature and the weather forecast – though that was very impor-

1 twitchy: nervous **2** be swaddled in sth.: be wrapped in sth. **3** whittle: cut figures or patterns into wood **4** wardroom: room where officers can meet and spend time **5** briefing: meeting where people are given information and instructions (usu. to prepare them for an upcoming event/task) **6** scale: *(hier) Maßstab*

tant information. Sometimes we would be told about a flotilla[1] of Others who had been spotted and attacked from the air, just in case some of them had survived and might still be coming in our direction. Occasionally there would be some big-picture news about crops[2] failing or countries breaking down or coordination between rich countries, or some other emerging detail of the new world we were occupying since the Change. Sometimes there would be news of an attack in which Others had used new or unexpected tactics, or attacked in surprising strength. If Others ever got through, we were told about it. The room would go very quiet. We'd hear when, where, how many.

There was no news like that on my first day. We sat shuffling[3] and fidgeting[4] and then the Captain came in. We stood up: not to attention[5], but we stood up. The Captain ran a tight company; there were lots of posts where nobody bothered to do that. He nodded and we sat down again and the room became still.

'Nothing special today,' he said. 'No sightings of Others reported from the air or sea. No news of any relevance from the wider world. It's two degrees now, high of five later, which will feel like about zero with the wind chill. Good news: we have a new Defender with us so we're back up to strength[6]. Kavanagh, stand up.'

I did. I looked around the room and all fourteen members of my squad looked back at me.

'He's starting his two years with us. Two years if he and you are lucky and we all do our jobs. Remember, the first few weeks, he's still training. Also remember, this isn't a drill[7]. We could be attacked today and he and you need to be ready. OK, that's it. I'll see you during my rounds.'

We stood up again and started to make for the door. The Sergeant came over to me and pointed in turn at a grumpy[8]-looking

1 flotilla: group of boats **2** crop: *Ernte* **3** shuffle: (here) move your feet nervously **4** fidget: move your body because you are nervous **5** (stand) to attention: the way soldiers stand when their superior talks to them **6** be back up to strength: have the full number of soldiers again **7** drill (n): (military) training **8** grumpy: bad-tempered

red-headed woman chewing gum sitting in the front row who'd been cleaning her fingers with a penknife during the briefing, the heavily bearded man who'd been sitting beside her, and a gender-indeterminate blob[1] in a balaclava[2] who'd been sitting behind me.

'Put him in the middle of you lot[3],' he said. 'Posts eight to fourteen. Hifa on the big gun. I'll come and see you there in thirty minutes.'

We went out onto the rampart[4] that led to the Wall. The Sergeant looked around at us and then he gave the order, the one which was once famous as the most frightening command in the army, the scariest sentence you would ever hear, because it was the immediate precursor of close combat; words which meant, there is a good chance that you will kill or die today. In the new world, it was a sentence Defenders heard at the start of every single shift. He said:

'Fix bayonets.'

And that's how it began.

1 blob: (here) plump mass **2** balaclava: woolen cap that covers head, neck and face **3** lot (n, infml): group of people **4** rampart: *Befestigungswall*

2

I think they used to call it concrete poetry, that thing where the words on the page look like a physical object, the object that the poem is trying to describe. You know, a poem about a tree in the shape of a tree, like this:

a
poem
about a
tree in the
shape of a tree,
in this case a Christ-
mas tree, not a very con-
vincing tree and not a very good
poem but it's not trying to be a death-
less masterpiece it's just to show the idea
yes?

A concrete poem. It feels an appropriate form for life on the Wall, because for a start life on the Wall is more like a poem than it is like a story. Days don't vary much; there isn't much a-to-b[1]. There isn't much narrative. You do have the constant prospect of action, the constant risk of sudden and total disaster – but that's not the same as stuff actually happening. Most days, it doesn't. The thing a typical day most resembles is the day before and the day after. It's less like a form of time and more like a physical element. Time as a thing, an object. And then because the Wall is the dominant thing in your life and the life of everyone else around you, and your responsibilities and your day and your thoughts are all about the Wall, and your

1 a-to-b (n, infml): movement from one place to another

future life is determined by what happens on the Wall – you can, fairly easily, lose your life here, or lose the life you wanted to have – the two entities[1] start to blur[2] together, Time and the Wall, Time and the Wall, the Wall and your day and your life sliding past, minute by minute.

Add in the fact that so much of the time, what you're mainly looking at is concrete. You stand on it, you sleep in it, your home and office and the place you eat and the place you shit and the place that gets in your dreams – concrete. Concrete ... there it is again. You could talk about the Wall in prose, or you could talk about it in poetry, but either way concrete would be prominent[3].

In prose it's a question of sheer scale[4]. The Wall is ten thousand kilometres long, more or less. (This country has a lot of coast.) It is three metres wide at the top, every centimetre of the way. On the sea side it is usually about five metres high; on the land side the height varies according to the terrain. There is a watch house every three kilometres: three thousand-plus of them. There are ramparts, stairs, barracks, exit points for boats, helipads[5], storage facilities, water towers, access structures, you name it. All of them made of concrete. If you had the stats[6] and the time and were sufficiently bored you could calculate just how much, but suffice it to say, that's a lot of concrete. Millions of tons of it. That's prose.

Prose is misleading, though, when it comes to saying what it feels and seems like. The days are the same, with variations in the weather, and the view is the same, with variations in the visibility, and the people either side of you are the same, so it's static; it's not a story, it's an image which is fixed-with-variations. It's a poem and as I already said, it's a concrete poem with a few repeating elements.

1 entity: thing **2** blur (v): become difficult to tell apart **3** prominent: important **4** scale: size **5** helipad: landing place for helicopters **6** stats (infml): statistics

One would be concrete itself:

concrete concrete concrete concrete concrete
concrete concrete concrete concrete concrete
concrete concrete concrete concrete concrete
concrete concrete concrete concrete concrete
concrete concrete concrete concrete concrete
concrete concrete concrete concrete concrete

But then there's also water, sky, wind, cold. Always water, sky, wind, cold, and of course concrete, so it's sometimes concretewaterskywindcold, when they all hit you as one thing, as a single entity, combined, like a punch, concretewaterskywindcold. Except it isn't always like that and you sometimes are affected by them distinctly, as separate things, and in a different order, so it might be

cold:::concrete:::wind:::sky:::water

or sometimes it's slower than that, they take time to sink in, so it might be a freak[1] clear calm day (they happen, not often, but they happen), in which case it's like an even shorter haiku

sky!
cold
water
concrete
wind

and then sometimes your perceptions slow, especially when it's cold, deep cold, and you're already tired, and it's towards the end of a watch, and then it's more like

1 freak (adj): unusual

cold
concrete
cold
water
cold
sky
old
wind
cold

Ah yes, the cold. The physical feeling of being on the Wall varies all the time, but varies within a narrow framework. It's always cold, but there is more than one type of cold, you soon learn, type 1 and type 2. Type 1 cold is the kind that's always there. It begins when you wake up in the barracks, as I did on that first day, and it's already cold, and it stays cold while you wash and use the toilet and put on your day clothes, layering up[1] from thermal underclothes, inner layers, outer layers, all your indoor gear[2], you go and eat, always porridge and sometimes protein and a warm drink, and you grab as many energy bars as you can face the thought of eating during the day before you go to the wardroom for a briefing, which sometimes has information about new threats but more usually tells you that today will be the same as yesterday, you go to the armoury and get your weapons, then get your outer layer of clothes on, windproofs and waterproofs and hat and gloves, everyone using a different rig[3] so by this point you look like the most disorganised army in the world, which in a way you are. Then you go out on the Wall and immediately you're hit by type 1 cold, the cold which is always already there, which you know so well and hate so much it's like being in one of those bands where they've been playing together for years and spent so much time together that they know each other so intimately that they can't bear to be in each other's company for

1 layer up: wear different layers of clothes **2** gear: (here) equipment **3** rig (n, infml): clothing

a second longer, they can identify each other blindfold[1] by the smell of each other's farts, and yet they have no choice because this, after all, is what they do and who they are. Then you walk to your post for the day (or the night if you're on night shift, which is exactly the same except twelve hours further on) and relieve the lucky sod[2] who is now off duty while you've become the poor sod who is on duty in their place. And by the time you've walked to your post, which can be a kilometre and a half away, you're generating some body heat and you've started to fight back against the cold and you realise that as long as you keep moving you're going to be just warm enough. That's type 1 cold.

Type 2 cold starts the same, except that as you move through it, it gets colder. After walking to your post for twenty minutes, you're colder than you were at the start. The cold gets through to you deeply and intimately. It feels dangerous because it is dangerous. People have died of hypothermia[3] on the Wall. You have no choice with type 2 cold except to keep moving as much as you can and, mainly, to try to find out in advance if it's going to be a type 2 day and plan accordingly. That means double layers of everything, double porridge, double warm drinks. Sometimes someone will run back to the barracks and bring more clothes, a big flask[4] of warm liquid, anything. I've even heard of units where they make fires and gather round them on the coldest nights, but the Captain would never let us get away with that. Type 1 cold can come to seem familiar, almost friendly, because you get to know it so well – the rest of your life, any time you feel cold, it will remind you of the Wall, and of this kind of cold, and because you're now remembering being miserable at a time when you're less miserable (by definition, you're less miserable, since you're no longer on the Wall), it will be not exactly a happy memory, but a memory with a happy effect: hooray, I'm no longer on the Wall! Somebody said there was no greater misery than recalling a time of happiness when you're in a time of despair, and that's true,

1 blindfold (adj): with covered eyes **2** sod (BE, infml, derog): guy **3** hypothermia [ˌhaɪpəˈθɜːmiə]: *Unterkühlung* **4** flask: bottle, (here) *Thermosflasche*

but let's focus on the positive and remember that the opposite is also true. When you remember the bad place, and you're no longer in the bad place, it feels good, like waking from a nightmare.

There are no positive thoughts about type 2. It cuts and slices and seeps[1] into you. The other cold feels like something outside you that you have to cope[2] with and overcome; type 2 feels internal. It gets inside your body, inside your head. It displaces part of you; it makes you feel as if there's less of you. Type 1 you can fight by moving, you can fight by thinking about something else. Type 2, there is nothing else. At times there's not even you. Type 1 people complain about. Type 2 makes them go silent, even afterwards. Type 2 is a premonition[3] of death.

That first day was a type 1 day. We climbed out on the ramp and started down the Wall towards our posts. Cold, horribly cold, but not dangerously so. Cold and medium clear. You can always tell the visibility on the Wall by how many watchtowers you can see. That day I could see the next two but not the third: they're three K[4] apart so that meant six kilometres but not nine. Call it seven. Medium visibility. It's the first thing you check because it tells you how far off you'll be able to spot Others. Clear days are better, unless you are looking into the sun at sunrise or sunset, in which case they're neither better nor worse. Attacks often come at that time and from that angle – which would give the Others better odds[5], except we know that that is a time they're likely to be coming and so tend to be prepared. At least that's what you'd think. Of the attacks which succeed, though, about half happen at dawn or dusk.

My fellow Defenders grumbled and muttered and bitched[6] as we walked. The Wall has gravel[7] on the top, along some sections anyway, to help with grip in the wet. This was one of those sections. We crunched[8] as we trudged[9]. Every two hundred metres, somebody

1 seep into sb./sth.: flow slowly into sb./sth. **2** cope with sth.: deal with sth., get along with sth. **3** premonition: vague knowledge of sth. before it happens **4** K: kilometre(s) **5** odds (pl): chances **6** bitch (v, infml): say bad things about sb. not present **7** gravel: small stones **8** crunch (v): *schlurfen* **9** trudge: walk slowly because you are exhausted

stopped at their post, peeling off from the shrinking group and taking up position beside whoever had been on guard from the other squad. There were sometimes a few words of abuse[1] or relief, a mixture of Thank God and About Fucking Time; all of the Defenders leaving their posts looked grey with exhaustion. They walked heavily. One or two of the guards at the furthest posts were already walking back towards us, notwithstanding[2] the fact that we hadn't got to them yet and their stations were technically unmanned in the interval. They wouldn't have done that if the Captain had been there, and if he had seen them he would have automatically added a day to their time on the Wall.

It was already light. The sun was low but, thanks to the layer of cloud, not dazzling[3].

The posts were numbered in faded white paint at hundred-metre intervals. Each post had a concrete bench, big enough for two people, facing the sea. The bearded man stopped at 8, the woman he'd been sitting next to – maybe they were in a relationship, there was something about their unspeaking ease with each other – took 10. At 12, Hifa, the blob in the balaclava, pointed at me and said, 'Here,' and kept walking on towards the next station, 14, the last one attached to our watch house. The Defender who'd been at my post, a bulky[4] man of about my height, picked up his rucksack and slung[5] his rifle over his shoulder and walked away without a word or gesture.

I took off my backpack and put it against the rampart. I stood and looked out at the sea. Twelve hours here felt like it was going to be a very very long time. Some companies divide their time into two shifts of six, but our Captain was one of the old-school ones who were more binary[6] about it: you're on or you're off. That seemed

1 abuse (n): (here) insults **2** notwithstanding sth. (fml): despite sth.
3 dazzling: so bright that you cannot see **4** bulky: heavy **5** sling sth. (slung – slung): throw sth. **6** binary ['baɪnəri]: belonging to a numerical system working only with 0 and 1, (here) allowing only two clearly distinct possibilities

like the worst idea in the world right now, but I knew that in eleven hours and fifty-five minutes I'd be all in favour.

Although everybody always calls the Wall the Wall, that isn't its official name. Officially it is the National Coastal Defence Structure. On official documents it's abbreviated to NCDS. Guard towers have a name and a number. This tower was Ilfracombe 4. We were on the outermost stretch of a long coastal curve. Straight in front, and for the ninety degrees to each side, there was nothing to see except the ocean. If straight in front was twelve o'clock, it was nothing but water from nine o'clock to three o'clock. Turn a further ten degrees to either side – turn to eight o'clock or four o'clock – and you could see the Wall undulating[1] into the distance. The engineers who built it tried to keep it as straight as possible, because straighter = shorter, but there were many places where the natural shape of what used to be the coastline meant that it was more economical, in time and effort and concrete, to use the existing shape of the coast as the guideline for the Wall. This must be one of them. My new home.

1 undulate [ˈʌndjuleɪt]: move like a wave

3

In every walk of life[1], every job and vocation[2], there is an experience which distinguishes actually doing the thing from the training and preparation, however extensive. You don't know what boxing is until somebody punches you, you don't know what doing a shift in a factory feels like until the bell has gone at the end of the day, you don't know what a day's march with a full backpack is until you've done one, and you don't know what the Wall means until you've stood a twelve-hour watch.

Time has never passed as slowly as it did that day. Time on the Wall is treacle[3]. Eventually, after you have put in enough hours on the Wall, you learn to cope with time. You train yourself not to look at the time, because it is never, never, ever, as late as you think and hope and long for it to be. You learn to float[4]. You become completely passive; you let the day pass through you, you stop trying to pass through it. But it takes months before you can do that. In the first weeks, and especially on your first day, you look at the time every few minutes. It's like there is a special slow time on the Wall; you can't believe it; you check and check again and that only makes it worse.

After two hours, at nine o'clock, a member of the kitchen staff brings around a hot drink. Sometimes it's tea, sometimes coffee, but really, who cares? It's a hot drink, it's a sign that you've done your first two hours. Somebody comes round on a bike, bringing a big heated flask. That first day, it was a woman, one of the cooks, who came along the Wall. I watched her stop for a minute or two at each post as she came. She was chatting with the Defenders. I felt my eyes fill with tears: the thought that someone was going to stop

1 walk of life: social position **2** vocation: job you strongly identify with
3 treacle ['tri:kl]: *Sirup* **4** float: move in the air or on water

and talk to me suddenly seemed like the greatest act of compassion[1] and empathy I had ever encountered[2]. As she got to the post before mine, where the woman next to me was on guard, I could hear both of them laughing. The sound of laughter on the Wall – it felt like an intrusion from another world. And I'd only been there two hours.

'Hello darling, I'm Mary,' said the cook, as she stopped her bicycle next to me, her curly hair peeking out from under her cap. 'Got your mug?'

I hadn't. I put my rifle down on the bench and got the standard-issue tin mug[3] out of my backpack. She poured hot brown liquid out of the flask.

'First day, isn't it? Poor thing. It always hits people hard. You get used to it though. And at least it's not raining or blowing a gale[4] or night-time so there's always that.'

'I'm Kavanagh,' I said. The liquid was dark brown tea, stewed and bitter, with so much sugar in, it was as sweet as ice cream. I had never drunk anything so delicious.

'I know you are, darling. Well, we'll be seeing each other at least three more times today, so we mustn't wear out[5] all the chat now. Keep 'em peeled[6]!'

And with that Mary was back on her bike, heading off towards Hifa, who had already put down the rocket launcher and turned to her in expectation. I kept watching while I drank my tea. It occurred to me that if the Others were able to work out a way of attacking during a tea break, their odds would be good. Mary got to Hifa and they gave each other a quick, very unmilitary hug. Mary got off her bike and leant it against the bench. Then she poured out Hifa's tea and awarded herself a mug too and they settled down to talking. I was jealous. Mary didn't seem to be worried about wearing out the chat when she was talking to Hifa, did she? They talked for about

1 compassion: sympathy, pity **2** encounter sb./sth.: meet sb./sth. **3** standard-issue tin mug: regular type of cup made of metal **4** gale: very strong wind **5** wear out sth.: use up sth. **6** keep (your eyes) peeled (infml): keep your eyes open

five minutes and then Mary got back on her bike and pedalled back down the top of the Wall, with a little wave for each one of us as she went past. It was three hours until lunch. I decided to break the time up into two sections of ninety minutes, with an energy bar in the middle.

'They put something in the tea to stop you thinking about sex,' somebody said on the communicator.

'Yeah,' said somebody else. 'They put tea.'

The next ninety minutes went past slowly, but not as slowly as the first two hours had done. I said to myself: maybe I'm starting to get the hang[1] of this Wall. Mistake. Having done some maths to make myself feel depressed the night before – two years on the Wall if I'm lucky – I now did some maths to cheer myself up. Two years = 730 days but it's two weeks on, two weeks off, so that's really only 365, and a day is really only a shift, since if the Others attack during somebody else's shift it's not your problem, so that's 365 shifts of twelve hours each, which by another way of looking at it is 187.5 full days, which is only six months, so my two years on the Wall is really only six months on the Wall, which isn't so bad.

After eighty-four minutes, I started counting down towards my power bar. 360 seconds, 359, 358 ... all the way down to 1. I took the waxed paper oblong[2] out of my upper left pocket and unwrapped it slowly, trying to take my time. The bars they give you on the Wall aren't labelled so you don't know what's inside them. Lucky dip[3]. This one was nutty and dense, with what seemed to be particles of red fruits, chewy and sweet and acidic[4], dotted[5] through it. I don't normally pay much attention to what I eat, but on the Wall, where for a lot of the time there isn't much to think about, I became obsessed with food. This power bar, for instance, was unlike anything else I had ever eaten – more intense, more important. The nuts had a different texture from the fruit. The bar was chewy and

1 get the hang of sth. (infml): understand sth. **2** oblong (n): rectangular shape **3** lucky dip: good choice **4** acidic [ə'sɪdɪk]: sour **5** be dotted through sth.: be contained in sth. in small bits

dry but also soft. Objectively and soberly[1], you would have to say that it was fairly nasty. Maybe you could go so far as to say it was horrible. At the same time it was the best thing I'd ever eaten. I tried to eat slowly, chewing each bite for as long as I could, thirty chews, forty, fifty, the flavours changing as I chewed, the fruits taking over from the nuts. I was glad when there was still three quarters of the bar left, calm when there was only half left, starting to feel regretful when I'd got down to the last quarter, then the last eighth, then the last mouthful, no crumbs left in the wrapper because the bar was too densely constructed for that, even when I tipped it up into my mouth, chewing fifty times, fifty-one, fifty-two, see if I can get to sixty, nope, there's nothing left, nothing in my mouth except saliva[2] and a faint tang[3] of dried raspberries.

When I looked up from the bar, the Captain was about a hundred metres away, walking towards me. I say 'walking': that was significant. Most of us trudged or shuffled along the Wall, and almost everyone, almost all the time, moved with their heads down. We all of us spent enough time looking out at the sea. You put off as long as you could the moment when you had to turn your attention outwards. Head down, eyes down. Nothing good to see if you look up.

The Captain wasn't like that. He stood straight and looked around him when he walked – or at least most of the time he did. On this occasion he was looking directly at me. He was wearing his uniform outers[4], which were bright green, because the Defenders' uniform is the opposite of camouflage[5]: instead of trying to hide from an enemy, we're trying to be as visible as possible, to the Others and to ourselves. The idea is that it will scare them and reassure us. The Captain for his part certainly did look scary enough, or reassuring enough, depending on your point of view.

1 soberly: *nüchtern* **2** saliva (n): liquid produced in your mouth **3** tang (n): taste **4** uniform outers: vest (usu. with pockets) worn on the top layer of a military uniform **5** camouflage: *Tarnkleidung*

I took my eyes off him and pretended to scan the horizon. Nothing to see. I wouldn't have minded a boatload of Others, just to break the suspense.

'Kavanagh,' he said when he arrived. His voice was deep and naturally severe – he was one of those men whose default mode[1] sounds like an order or a rebuke[2].

'Sir.'

'We're here to look out at the sea,' he said. I took that to mean he had seen my long absorption in my midmorning snack. The Wall is not a place where people blush, but I felt myself flush red.

'Sorry sir.'

He stopped staring at me and turned to look at the water. Concrete sky wind water. A few moments passed. Directly above us I could see the contrails[3] of a plane. Energy is plentiful, thanks to nuclear power, but fuel isn't, especially not aviation fuel, so now only very few people get to go on planes. That would be members of the elite, flying off to talk to other members of the elite about the Change and the Others and what to do about them. At least that's what they say they do. I felt the familiar longing to be up there, one of them, instead of down here, one of us. The Captain and I both watched the plane move into the distance. If he had been a different kind of person, he would have spat.

'Everyone finds the first day hard. The second is easier. The third easier still. Eventually you get the measure of it.' He turned to me again.

'This is my fourth tour on the Wall. No Other has ever got over the Wall on my duty. I've never lost a company member. I don't intend those things to change.' He looked at me again to make sure I got the point, then nodded and marched off towards Hifa at the end of our section of Wall.

1 default mode: standard mode, (here) usual tone of sb.'s voice **2** rebuke (n): act of speaking aggressively to sb. who did sth. wrong **3** contrail (n): line left in the sky by a plane

I thought: he's an impressive man, our Captain. He's a leader. Four turns on the Wall: that meant he had done three supplementary[1] tours of duty[2], each one of which earned perks[3] and privileges for himself and his family. Better house, better food, better schools for his children. They say this is one of the ways people rise up and become members of the elite. So, a family man. A brave man, a family man, a leader, an athlete. A person with a sense of duty and responsibility. A good man to follow into battle. If you had asked me right then and there what was the least likely thing I could think of about the Captain, it would be that he was also, above and beyond any other thing, the biggest fucking liar I've ever met.

1 supplementary: additional **2** tour of duty: military service **3** perk: extra money or benefits

4

I took so long over my power bar and my chat with the Captain that the ninety minutes until lunch was actually only eighty minutes. I started to get the hang of the fact that looking at the time made it pass by more slowly. Another plane went past, heading in the other direction this time – more members of the elite, coming and going, talking their talk. Oh how wonderful it would be to be up in the air ... The wind rose, not to gale force but to something a little stronger than a breeze, and the sea swell[1] was both rolling and choppy[2]. The sky cleared and I could now see four watchtowers: visibility twelve kilometres. I began to understand just how hard it could be to see what was in the water, even on a clear day, when the wind and waves and sun did not cooperate.

The drill at lunch varies from watchtower to watchtower. At Ilfracombe 4 the routine is that people are allowed to gather together for ten minutes with the two defenders in the nearest posts. The furthest anyone is from their post is two hundred metres; the biggest gap between a group having lunch is six hundred metres. Safe enough to have a gap of that size for ten minutes twice a day. You'd have thought. At three minutes to twelve, I saw Hifa at post 14 put down the grenade launcher and take something out of his or her rucksack, then pick up the weapon again and begin walking towards me. I turned and looked the other way and the red-haired woman from post 10 was heading towards me as well.

They arrived at the same time and both of them sat down on the bench without speaking. They put down their weapons and started opening their packed lunches. The woman pulled back the hood of her outer coat, and I could see some strands of red hair escaping

1 swell (n): rising and falling movement of the sea **2** choppy: not calm

from underneath her beanie[1]. She looked less irritable[2] than she had earlier in the day. Not a morning person. Hifa was still entirely wrapped up, and all I could see was the eyes and the tip of the nose. If you had asked me beforehand, I would have said it was impossible to eat a meal without taking off your balaclava, but that was clearly what was about to happen.

I got my food out too and sat down at the end of the bench.

'So how's it going, new meat?' asked the woman.

'Kavanagh,' I said, sticking out my hand. Both of us still had gloves on. She gave it a quick firm shake.

'Simpson,' she said. 'Or Shoona.'

'Shoona. It's OK. The Captain caught me staring at my power bar.'

'Yeah, he does that. Catches people. That right, Hif?'

Hifa grunted, mouth full.

'Wouldn't you rather have lunch with ...?' I said, and gestured towards the man she'd been sitting next to at breakfast. He was in the next group of three, four hundred metres away. Shoona shrugged.

'You know what they say. For better, for worse[3], but never for lunch.'

Hifa snorted a laugh.

'You're Breeders?'

This time both of them laughed.

'No of course we're not fucking Breeders. Do I look like a Breeder? Don't answer that. Cooper and I are just having sex.'

'You like him,' said Hifa, at some point equidistant[4] between a statement and a question and a tease. I was sorry to hear the question, because what I wanted to ask was something else: where did they have sex? There was no privacy on the Wall. Only Breeders (i.e. people trying to be Breeders) and officers got separate accommodation. The showers?

1 beanie: loose-fitting hat made of cotton or wool **2** irritable: becoming angry easily **3** for better, for worse: *wohl oder übel* **4** equidistant (adj): equally far away from two points, right in the middle between two points

'Well enough,' said Shoona. 'More than I like this sodding[1] sandwich, anyway.'

It was hard to disagree with that. The sandwich bread was dry and what was supposed to be a layer of cream cheese was thin-to-invisible. The food on the Wall is pretty good, on the whole; they take trouble over it because they know how important it is in a Defender's twelve-hour shift.

'Chewy,' I said. For some reason that was very very funny. Both of them bent over, cackling[2], thumping themselves first on the legs, then on each other's backs.

'True,' said Shoona, when she got her breath back. She took a long pull from her bottle of water. 'Well, Chewy, time to get back to it. This Wall's not gonna guard itself.'

We put our lunch stuff away and picked up our weapons and Shoona and Hifa started trudging back to their posts. Hifa got about five metres away and then turned around and said, 'See ya, Chewy.'

Once Hifa and Shoona had got back to their posts, I let a few minutes go past before I looked at my watch. I was starting to learn. It was now twelve thirty. The good news was I had got through five and a half hours. The bad news was that I had six and a half more to go. With the sun higher in the sky, it was easier to see now, meaning that this should be a time of less risk. The Others knew that too, which meant that you couldn't rely on it. If everyone knows it's a time of low risk, maybe that's a good moment to try something. So low risk is high risk. But not vice versa[3].

Mornings on the Wall, dawn and dusk and night, were times for poetry. Skyconcretewaterwind. Afternoons were for prose. Ten thousand kilometres of Wall. A Defender for every two hundred metres: fifty thousand Defenders on duty at any time. Another fifty thousand on the other shift, so a hundred thousand on duty, day in day out. Plus it's two weeks on, two weeks off. Half of the Defenders aren't on the Wall, they're on leave or on training or waiting for their

1 sodding (adj, sl): damn **2** cackle: laugh loudly **3** vice versa (adv): the other way around

two weeks' turn of duty. So two hundred thousand active Defenders at any given moment. Add support and ancillary staff[1], officers and administrators, add the Coast Guard and the air force and the navy, people off sick, whatever, and it's more than three hundred thousand people involved in defending the Wall. That's why everybody goes to the Wall, no exceptions. That's the rule.

Except for Breeders. It's a paradox. Because the Wall needs so many people, we need people to Breed[2], so that there are enough people to man[3] the Wall. It's on a fine edge[4] as things currently stand, and there's talk of the tours having to be made longer, two and a half or three years, to make up a shortfall[5]. But people don't want to Breed, because the world is such a horrible place. So as an incentive[6] to get people to leave the Wall, if you reproduce, you can leave. You Breed to leave the Wall. Some people say that this isn't fair to the children, who are born into a world where they have to do time[7] on the Wall in their turn. Maybe they won't, though. Maybe all the Others will have died off by then and we won't need the Wall. Who knows? And besides, the children can always Breed in their turn, and get off the Wall that way. Prolonging the life of our species too, as a side effect. Breed to Leave, that's the slogan.

I should say that people don't despise[8] or look down on Breeders. They just think they're a bit weird. It's not so much, that's wrong, it's more, why would you? Why don't people want to Breed? It's an idea that caught on[9] after the Change: that we shouldn't want to bring children into the world. We broke the world and have no right to keep populating[10] it. We can't feed and look after all the humans there already are, here and now; the humans who are here and now, most of them, are starving and drowning, dying and desperate; so how dare we make more of them? They aren't starving and drowning here, in this country, but they are almost everywhere else; so

1 ancillary staff [æn'sɪləri stɑːf]: *Hilfspersonal* **2** breed (v): produce offspring **3** man sth. (v): provide people for sth. **4** be on a fine edge: have just enough resources for sth. **5** shortfall: shortage **6** incentive (n): motivation **7** do time (v): serve time **8** despise sb./sth.: strongly dislike sb./sth. **9** catch on (infml): become accepted or popular **10** populate sth.: inhabit sth., occupy sth.

how dare we make more humans to come into this world? There are lots of different answers to that. Nobody can predict the future; that's one answer. God tells us to; that's an answer which works for some. Maybe the best answer, though, or maybe I'm just talking about the one that makes the most sense to me, is just, because[1]. Because; the best/worst answer to most human questions. Why are we here? Because.

Back to the prose. Most Defenders stand on the Wall because that's where the manpower is needed, but the Wall isn't the only form of border and coastal protection. The Flight scans the seas for Others, locates them, sometimes 'takes them out' then and there. It's funny, only Defenders on the Wall talk about 'killing' Others: we're the ones who do it face to face, and we're the only ones who don't use euphemisms[2] for it. The Flight consists of some people in planes and many more people operating drones. Sometimes the Flight marks their location for the Guards, full name Coast Guards but everyone calls them Guards, who use ships of two main kinds, medium-range and short-range. They patrol the coast and the seas and their job is to sink the Others' boats. The Defenders are there for the rest of the Others: the ones who get through, which is a significant number, because there is a lot of sky and sea to watch, and because ten thousand kilometres of coast is a lot of coast. They come in rowing boats and rubber dinghies[3], on inflatable tubes, in groups and in swarms and in couples, in threes, in singles; the smaller the number, often, the harder to detect. They are clever, they are desperate, they are ruthless[4], they are fighting for their lives, so all of those things had to be true for us as well. We had to be clever and desperate and ruthless and fight for our lives, only more so, or we would switch places. I didn't want to die fighting on the Wall, but if it came to it, I would rather that than be put to sea[5]. One in, one out: for every Other who got over the Wall, one Defender would be

1 (just) because: (here) for no particular reason **2** euphemism: expression that makes a bad thing sound good **3** dinghy: small boat **4** ruthless: cruel **5** put sb. to sea: abandon sb. on the sea

put to sea. A tribunal of our fellow Defenders would convene[1] and decide who was most responsible, and those people, in that order of responsibility, would be put in a boat that same day. If five Others got over the Wall, five of us would be put to sea. It was easy to imagine being those people. Your old comrades pointing guns at you while you pushed your boat out into the water, the only feeling colder and lonelier and more final than being on the Wall.

Members of the Flight and the Guard don't get put to sea, so people would rather do that than be on the Wall. As a result it's much harder to get in. To get into the Flight you have to pass lots of biomechanical tests. (I wear glasses so I didn't even bother applying. I learnt afterwards that was a mistake, because the Flight has lots of ground staff and support staff and I could have got a job there.) To get into the Guard it helps to have family connections with boats and the sea. I didn't bother applying for that either, because I've hardly ever been on a boat and I was worried I'd get seasick. No, it was the Wall for me. It was always going to be the Wall.

That first afternoon went by slowly. Planes passed overhead a few times; once, about two o'clock, I saw a boat on the horizon, got excited and called it in[2], but I was shouted down by my fellow Defenders, who said it was a Guard ship. They said they could tell by the shape. After Yos finished calling me an idiot over the communicator, Sarge came on and told me I would soon be able to recognise Guard ships on sight and that it was better to call in something I didn't know about than keep quiet and risk something worse. I felt better after that. At three, I had another power bar, this time made of savoury[3] ingredients, chickpeas[4] I think and maybe sesame and carrot. It wasn't especially nice but I was glad of it, and more glad of Mary's second visit on her bike with her flask of hot liquid, coffee this time.

'Nearly there,' she said, as she pedalled off. But that wasn't true, and the last few hours went by just as heavily as the rest of the day.

1 convene: hold a meeting **2** call sth. in: *(hier) etw. melden* **3** savoury: salty
4 chickpea: *Kichererbse*

It began to get dark at around five. The day had clouded over. It was one of those evenings which seem not so much a transition from day to night as from light grey to thicker grey to darker grey to darker still, the light fading by increments[1], until dark wins. Lights came on automatically, a hundred metres apart on the Wall. The lamps threw a narrow patch of blazing illumination which only made the dark around more intense. Some sections of the Wall were said to disable their lights and use night-vision instead; I could see why. There was no moon. I suddenly realised just how hard it would be to see Others coming at night, if the weather and light conditions were at all difficult. I also realised why they always start you on the Wall on a day shift: so you've had a chance to get used to a twelve-hour stint[2] of duty before you have to do one when it really matters, at night, when the Others come.

For the first time that day, I grew anxious, not about fatigue[3] or cold or whether I would get through it, but about the Others. It was not difficult to imagine a black-clad[4] figure hopping silently over the Wall, knife in its hand, murder in its eyes, nothing to lose. No warning; no mercy. I tried to look straight ahead and then move my head from side to side, using my peripheral vision[5], the way we had been trained to do. All I could think of was how easy it would be for the Others if they attacked now.

'Different at night, isn't it?' said a voice into my ear. I looked across and could see Hifa looking towards me. I raised an arm in acknowledgement.

'You get used to it,' Hifa added. 'Sort of.'

The wind dropped at dusk, and the swell settled down. I could hear a motorboat in the distance. One of ours, I assumed – no Others would mount[6] an assault in something so noisy. It would be a Guard patrol going home after dark. I could hear a plane far overhead too; that would be the Flight, also on their way home. The wind

1 by increments: step by step **2** stint: time period you spend on a job
3 fatigue [fəˈtiːg]: exhaustion **4** black-clad: dressed in black **5** use peripheral vision: *aus dem Augenwinkel sehen* **6** mount sth. (v): (here) begin sth.

and the waves were quieter now, but I was more aware of them, because they were less constant. I started to think I could hear patterns in the sound, whispering or singing or voices muttering not-quite-words. An image began to run through my mind, not quite a hallucination or a waking dream, but like a guided fantasy, like the kind of story you tell yourself in the liminal[1] in-between consciousness just as you're falling asleep or just after you've woken up. The noises, the near-voices, were being made by a choir, hooded and robed in black, chanting[2] in a ritual, appeasing[3] spirits or gods or demons or the ancestors[4]. There were two rows of them and their faces were in shadow, and maybe they themselves didn't know the meaning of what they were chanting. Maybe it was a dirge[5], a funeral dirge. They were monks or nuns or a mixture of the two. They were chanting because they wanted something to happen, or not to. The chanting was a lament[6] or a prayer.

'Here they come,' said the Sergeant over the communicator. I was so woozy[7], so out of it, that my first thought was that the black-robed figures were coming, had leapt out of my imagination and were here on the Wall with us. The adrenaline helped me snap out of it: he meant, the night shift was coming. The next shift of our company had come out of the watchtower and were clumping[8] down the ramparts towards us. I don't think I've ever felt my mood flip so abruptly and completely. Relief broke over me like a great wave. Relief is maybe the purest form of happiness there is; in that moment, anyway, I'd have said so. I'd never been happier; I'd never been more purely and ecstatically in the present. Cold? What cold? Here comes the next shift! Slowly, admittedly, very slowly, heads down, trudging and grumbling, the same way we had twelve hours ago. Take your time, guys, I thought, take it as slow as you like, as long as you keep coming.

1 liminal (adj): on the border between two states of being **2** chant (v): sing **3** appease sb.: make sb. calm and friendly towards you **4** ancestor: person in your family who lived before you **5** dirge: sad song, song of mourning **6** lament (n) [lə'ment]: sad song **7** woozy (fml): dizzy, confused **8** clump (v): walk making a lot of noise with your feet

There was no ceremony and not much small talk at the moment of handover. The Defender I'd seen twelve hours before arrived at my post. He was chewing gum. He did not speak but instead flicked[1] his head up at me in a combination of greeting and dismissal. I already had my pack on and my rifle slung over my shoulder. I flicked my head back at him and started the walk back to the watchtower and the barracks. I realised that I had stiffened up with the cold and immobility. My legs hurt from standing. The wind, which had got up again, was directly in my face. It felt like it didn't matter. The shift was over. That was the only thing that counted.

When you're on the Wall, the division of time is very simple. Twelve hours on duty, twelve hours off. In practice that means four hours for you, eight hours for sleep. I don't really remember what I did that first evening, but I do still remember the physical sensation of coming in out of the cold, aching[2] with fatigue, and taking my pack off and dropping my rifle at the armoury and then just sitting, sitting in the dry and the warmth, and thinking that I had never really appreciated sitting before, had never fully got the point of it, but that now I did, and I would never again underestimate how good it is to have nothing to do, no demands on you, except to sit. Most of the patrol sat around too. We were in the mess hall. There was tea and biscuits – the best tea, the best biscuits. Nobody spoke much, or made a great deal of sense when they did. Then there was hot food – I don't remember what, but I do remember going back for thirds[3]. Some of the shift went to clean up, others to call home and check in with whoever it was they'd left behind. A few of us were gaming on our communicators, a few went through to watch television. I did all of those things in sequence and then woke with Yos shaking my shoulder.

'You fell asleep,' he said. 'Daft[4] bugger[5], you might have been here all night,' his tone kinder than his words. The TV was on but the

1 flick: make a quick movement **2** ache (v): feel pain **3** for thirds: for a third portion **4** daft (adj, infml): stupid **5** bugger (sl, derog): guy

room was empty; it was a chat show with the sound turned right down. He laughed. 'The first one is a long one. Bedtime.'

I followed him through to the barracks bedroom. There were different generations of design at different points along the Wall; some watchtowers had individual bedrooms. This design, with everyone in one big room, was from a period when the theory was that Defenders should share things, so that they understand they're all in it together. My shift was in bed or getting ready for it, the other shift's beds were empty. It was the same as when I'd arrived only the day before, though that fact – that it was only twenty-four hours since I had walked into this room – made no sense. It felt more like twenty-four years. I washed, stripped off my day clothes, then put on my night clothes, starting with a thermal inner layer. The lights went out.

I took off my glasses and got into bed. But then I realised there was one last thing I wanted to do before going to sleep. I put my glasses back on and got back out of bed. I walked down to the far end of the barracks. Most of the squad was already asleep, one or two of them snoring. Someone, I couldn't tell who, was reading under the blankets with the help of a penlight[1]. The moon had risen by now and some sharp light was coming in the narrow high windows. I stopped at the last cubicle beside the washroom. I looked down and saw what I was looking for: caramel-coloured skin and short waved hair and a button nose peering over the thickly stacked[2] blankets. I thought I had got away with it, but just as I turned, I saw that Hifa's eyes were open, looking narrowly at me, glinting[3] and amused. But I had got what I wanted.

Hifa was a woman. I went back to bed, and that was my first day on the Wall.

1 penlight: flashlight **2** stack (v): put on top of each other **3** glint (v): sparkle, shine

5

On the Wall, one day is every day. At least, it is in terms of the big-picture items[1] such as the shape of the twenty-four hours, your duties, where you go and what you do and who you do it with. Lots of variation within that, but the architecture of the days is the same. That's the way you want it to be, too, because on the Wall, any news is bad news. They're never going to say, guess what, the Others have stopped coming and you can leave the Wall now. Guess what, we've decided we like your face and you don't have to do two years on the Wall, in fact you can leave tomorrow, in fact, wait, why not, you can leave right this minute! Off you go! Wait, you forgot your cookies!

That's not going to happen. The only things that can happen are bad things. So you want nothing to happen. Except it's more complicated than that. Somewhere in the dark cave-mind there's a gremlin[2], saying, But wouldn't it be interesting if something did happen, if they came, if you had to fight for your life, if you had to do that thing you dread[3] and train for, have nightmares about but maybe just are a tiny bit curious about too, and you have to kill or be killed? Wouldn't it be better to do that, to feel something other than cold and hunger and boredom and fatigue? Wouldn't it be exciting to use that bayonet you clamp on your gun every morning? You'll get to find out something about yourself, what you are like when the worst happens. Whether you are still you.

Only the louder and stupider Defenders will ever talk about this, but we all think about it. We half-fantasise about the worst that could happen.

Mostly, though, what happens is nothing, and mostly, that's the way we like it. My first two weeks on the Wall were like that. Every

1 big-picture item: main thing, main point **2** gremlin: (imaginary) little monster
3 dread sb./sth.: fear sb./sth.

day was the same as the first day, with the main variable being the weather. Most days were about as cold as the first. Two were warmer – not warm enough to be warm but warm enough to go out with one layer less. One day was type 2 cold, dangerously cold, frighteningly cold, but the weather forecasters had told us it was coming and we were prepared. The really lethal[1] cold is the kind that comes on when you aren't expecting it.

I saw the same people every day, the members of my squad. I walked out to the wall with Shoona and Hifa and we had lunch together. The nickname Chewy, I am sorry to say, stuck. Yos and the Sergeant took turns pointing out things I was doing wrong, things I could do differently, things to watch out for. I realised that this was ongoing training, and though I didn't like being found fault with[2] all the time, I could see why they were doing it. Shoona began to tease me and Hifa about being an item[3], singing 'Hifa and Chewy sitting in a tree, k-i-s-s-i-n-g.' There was nothing personal about the teasing, it was almost pro forma: if a male Defender and a female Defender were in any way friendly to each other, if they were anything other than fridge-temperature indifferent, they could expect to be accused of being 'at it'. In this case, though, Shoona was on to[4] something, because I was starting to have thoughts about Hifa. Even though I had never seen her in anything other than multiple layers of baggy clothing. Actually, maybe that was part of what was getting my attention – looking at all those shapeless clothes, it was hard not to wonder about the shape underneath them … formlessness which you know isn't really formlessness, which you know for sure has a definite shape, an unmistakable glow … and also, it is a conclusive human truth that the only thing which makes the time pass better than daydreaming about food is daydreaming about sex. So, yes, Hifa and Chewy, but not necessarily sitting in a tree, k-i-s-s-i-n-g.

1 lethal [ˈliːθl]: deadly **2** find fault with sb./sth.: criticize sb./sth. **3** item (infml): (here) couple **4** be on to sth.: suspect sth. that turns out to be true

One day the Sergeant properly yelled at me, when he made an impromptu[1] inspection and found that I didn't have my spare ammunition rigged[2] correctly. He was right: there was a particular manner in which we were supposed to do it, magazines folded back over each other in a set sequence, which made it quicker to load the ammo[3] in combat, but it was laborious[4] and boring to do, and so I sometimes skipped it.

There was nothing particularly unusual about being shouted at, so that wasn't the main point of interest. The thing which made me focus was what Sarge said when he'd calmed down a little.

'You're lucky it was me,' he said. 'The Captain sees that, you get extra days on the Wall. That thing you did right there, that's an extra two weeks on the watch. You want that?'

It didn't seem to be a rhetorical question. I had to admit that no, I did not want that.

'I didn't think so,' said Sarge. 'Most people, their bark is worse than their bite[5]. For pretty much everybody, that's true. Their bark is their bite. Yelling or bollocking[6] or calling you names is the worst they'll ever do. Not him. His bite is worse than his bark. You don't have to worry about him giving you a bollocking. You have to worry about him doing you real damage. Bite, not bark. Do you get it?'

I said that I thought I did. That didn't seem good enough, and Sarge came closer, confidentially close, as if we were in a crowded pub and he was whispering a secret, not as if we were on the Wall, in the middle of nowhere, two hundred metres from the nearest human ears.

'I'll tell you something about the Captain. It's not a secret, but it's something he prefers to tell people for himself. When he does tell you, do me a favour and act like it's a surprise.' He looked around, as if he was worried about eavesdroppers[7], and he lowered his voice

1 impromptu (adj): spontaneous **2** rig sth.: adjust sth., arrange sth. **3** ammo (infml): ammunition **4** laborious: complicated and tiresome **5** Their bark is worse than their bite: *Hunde, die bellen, beißen nicht* **6** bollocking (n): act of shouting at sb. you are angry with **7** eavesdropper: person secretly listening to what other people are saying

so that I could barely hear him over the wind. 'The Captain was an Other. He got here ten years ago, before the laws changed. That's why he's so hardcore. That's why he's so strict. He knows what it's like out there. He knows he's not going back. He's done four turns on the Wall because he's obsessed with keeping them out and proving he is worth being allowed to stay.' He let it sink in then hissed[1]: 'The Captain was an Other!'

It was one of those things you're told which make no sense and at the same time you immediately know, right down in your cells, are true. The Captain was an Other! Of course he was. Until about ten years ago, Others who showed they had valuable skills could stay, at the cost of exchanging places with the Defenders who had failed to keep them out. The law was changed because this fact became known to Others and started to act as a 'pull factor', a reason they came here. Now, today, Others who get over the Wall have to choose between being euthanised[2], becoming Help or being put back to sea. There's no escape and no alternative, now that everybody in the country has a chip: without one, you'd last about ten minutes. So even if they get over the Wall and then get away, they're always caught and offered the standard choice. Almost all of them choose to be Help. The attraction is that if they have children, the children are raised as citizens. That's after being taken away from their parents, of course. Others tend to be Breeders. You see the kids all around the place, often with older parents, or parents who are a visibly different ethnicity from their children. The Captain must have been one of the last to get through before the new laws. No wonder he was a fanatic. No wonder his bite was worse than his bark. His scars were tribal[3] scars, and yet he had left behind his tribe and was now a Defender, one of us.

'I get it,' I said to Sarge. 'I get it.' I refolded the magazines of ammunition, the way I had been taught to do it, while he watched. The Captain used to be an Other ... of course, of course, it made

1 hiss (v): *zischen* **2** euthanise sb.: kill sb. who is sick with a lethal dose of medicine **3** tribal (adj): *Stammes-*

complete sense. There was something abnormal about his implacability[1]. It was easier to understand once you started to think about the things he must have seen, the things he must have done. That day was the last time I cheated or took a short cut or cut a corner or did anything not one hundred per cent by the book[2]. I became Mr Rules. I realised that even though I was on the Wall, a part of me had been assuming there were still small human margins here and there, room for interpretation, space for forgiveness or acceptance or, less nobly, the chance to talk yourself out of any trouble you might have got yourself into. I now saw that that was wrong. No leeway[3], no space, nothing but black and white, the rulebook or anarchy, nothing but the Wall and the Others and the always waiting, always expectant, entirely unforgiving sea.

1 implacability [ɪmplækəˈbɪləti]: *Unerbittlichkeit* **2** by the book: according to the rules **3** leeway: degree of freedom you have to change a situation

6

After that first two-week shift on the Wall I went home. The trip was the reverse of the one I'd made to the Wall: lorry, train, second train, bus, walk. It might sound similar but it couldn't have been more different, and the main difference was that the whole company was travelling back with me. A company of thirty-plus, heading off together after two weeks of what amounted[1] to hard labour and semi-incarceration[2]. We were a little, I think the word would be, *rowdy*. No alcohol is allowed on the Wall, a strict rule strictly enforced: if you're caught you and anyone else involved, or thought to be involved, automatically get extra days to serve. Somehow, though, as soon as we were on the lorry, two-litre bottles of spirits magically appeared. We passed them around, swigging[3] happily, and again I felt the pure joy you sometimes got on the Wall, the joy of relief, when something horrible is over. One of life's great pleasures, deeply loved by all Defenders: the moment when you get to say: I hated that, but now it's finished.

This was the first chance I got to interact with the other shift. A strange thing: we were all in the same place at the same time, doing the same thing, but we hardly ever had anything to do with each other, apart from those few fumbling[4] moments of handover at either end of a watch. That could make you hate each other, because your emotions, at that moment, couldn't possibly be more out of sync[5]: starting a shift meant depressed, resentful[6], apprehensive, bitterly doing the worst thing in your life; finishing one meant euphoric, ecstatic, relieved, skipping off to the best bit of the day. Going off

1 amount to sth.: add up to sth. **2** semi-incarceration [ˈsemi ɪnˌkɑːsəˈreɪʃn]: partial imprisonment **3** swig (v, infml): drink **4** fumbling (adj): awkward **5** out of sync: not in agreement **6** resentful: angry

shift, you felt no ill-will[1] to your doppelgänger, but that wasn't true in reverse, because he hated you. In twelve hours it would be the other way around. Nothing personal: when you came on shift, you always hated the person you were relieving[2]. The fact that you knew the other set of emotions so completely, that you knew exactly what the other person was feeling, made it worse. Your shift twin was a person you met twice a day, about whom you had very strong views, whom you didn't really know.

After the lorry, we got on a train, a civilian train, which ran from the nearest town up to the capital. I felt sorry for the other passengers: we were loud, we were rude, we didn't care what anyone else thought or what they needed – this was our train. People were used to that kind of behaviour from Defenders, and tended to give us a lot of space. (Good idea.) When we piled into our carriage, a Breeder with a small child at the far end picked up her child and her bags and moved elsewhere. (Also good idea.) It was warm, indeed verging[3] on overheated, after the two weeks I'd spent on the Wall. I'd forgotten what it felt like to be hot; it was nice for the first couple of minutes, and then I could feel myself starting to sweat. We all took off multiple layers of clothing. There was yet more booze[4] – someone had taken the chance to pick up another couple of bottles at the station. We got stuck into the drinking. The train set off. Some of the company were singing. Shoona and Cooper, after two drinks, were sitting holding hands and occasionally, when they thought nobody was looking, kissing. You could see that they liked each other more than either let on[5]. I had found myself, not by chance, a seat next to Hifa at the end of the carriage. Hifa minus ten layers of clothing was lithe[6], skinny, tough and frail[7] at the same time. Her black hair stuck out in all directions. It was only about the third time I'd seen her without a beanie or cap. We were sitting there talking about nothing much, when a man, a Defender, came and dumped himself in the

1 ill-will (n): unfriendly feelings towards sb. **2** relieve sb.: take the position of sb. **3** verge on sth.: be very close to sth. **4** booze (infml): alcoholic beverages **5** let on sth.: confess sth. **6** lithe [laɪð]: *gelenkig* **7** frail: thin and weak

seat across from us and held out a bottle of vodka. I took it, nodded thanks, took a swig[1], handed it to Hifa, who took a swig and handed it back to the man. All through this he kept looking at me. Then I got it.

'You're him!'

He laughed. A hot waft of alcohol came across the train table. It was indeed him, my shift twin. It was no surprise I didn't recognise him, since he was another Defender I'd never seen out of his Wall clothes, swaddled in layers of cold-weather protection, wearing a beanie with a hood pulled down over it. Take four sets of outerwear off him, and he was a slim dark-haired man with brown eyes and a four-day beard. My age. That was to be expected, most Defenders were.

'Hughes,' he said.

'Kavanagh,' I said.

'Chewy,' he said.

'I don't love it, but I suppose so.'

'You're skinnier than I thought, Chewy.'

'Same. It's the—'

'Yeah, I know.'

'How long?'

'Fifty-eight weeks.'

In the middle. Hughes didn't ask how long I'd been on the Wall. He didn't need to because he knew first-hand. He started to get up.

'So, see you at training week. Just wanted to say hello.'

'Thanks. Yes.'

He stood by our seats for a moment and raised the bottle in a toast.

'Well, if you are going to Breed, you could both do worse.'

In unison, Hifa and I said: 'Fuck off.'

He laughed and headed off down the carriage towards the sing-along, him and the train both swinging and swaying from side to side. The company had run through the repertoire of old pop songs,

1 swig (n, infml): *Schluck*

switched to obscene favourites (which had emptied the carriage of the few remaining civilians – we now had it entirely to ourselves), and then started singing the all-time Defender classic, melancholy and defiant[1] and nihilistic all at once, not so much a song as a chant or dirge:

We're on the Wall because
We're on the Wall because
We're on the Wall because
We're on the Wall because [stamp three times, pause
for three beats]
We're on the Wall ...

and so on. The effect was hypnotic, self-transcending[2]; you never felt less of an individual, more of a group, than when you were singing that song/chanting that chant/dirging[3] that dirge. There was no sign that the song was going to stop, so Hifa and I, a few seats from the rest of the company, joined in. I can't sing, not even slightly, but with that particular song it doesn't matter. Hifa's singing voice was unexpectedly high and delicate. We're on the Wall because We're on the Wall, because ...

Night had settled, and the train windows were now half-opaque[4], so you could choose whether to look out the window into the dark landscape outside, or keep your focus on the reflection back into the train carriage. I've always liked that trick of perspective and perception. I alternated between the reflection and the view through the window. Moon, cows, trees, a river; my own face with Hifa behind me, the battered train fittings, the other Defenders, singing and swigging. The view beyond or the view within, the landscape or the reflection, inside or outside. The cold out there, the warmth in here.

1 defiant: insolent, provocative **2** self-transcending: going beyond the limits of the self **3** dirge (v): sing a sad song **4** opaque [əʊˈpeɪk]: impossible to see through

At London, we split up, after a certain amount of hugging and joshing[1], and carrying each other off the train, and throwing up. The company dispersed to take a variety of different trains to our various parts of the country. For me it was a short hop across town on the underground and then a two-hour stopping train[2] to the Midlands. This time I was the only Defender, and instead of running away to other compartments, people snuck looks[3] at me, until I looked back at them, and then they acted as if they'd been caught doing something they knew they shouldn't. Then it was a wait for the local bus, last one of the evening, then the bus, then a walk from the terminus[4], a mile or so but feeling longer with my rucksack and my emotions about home both bearing down on me. My parents had left the porch light on, so I could spot our house from a long way off, the only semi[5] in our street which was still illuminated on the outside. They'd be waiting up. I squared my shoulders and knocked on the door.

Home: it didn't just seem as if home was a long way away, or a long time ago, it actually felt as if the whole concept of home was strange, a thing you used to believe in, an ideology you'd once been passionate about but had now abandoned. Home: the place where, when you have to go there, they have to take you in. Somebody had said that. But once you had spent time on the Wall, you stop believing in the idea that anybody, ever, has no choice but to take you in. Nobody has to take you in. They can choose to, or not.

1 josh (v, infml): fool around **2** stopping train: local train that stops at a lot of stations **3** sneak a look at sb.: look secretly at sb. **4** terminus: last stop, end of the line **5** semi (n, infml): *Doppelhaushälfte*

7

None of us can talk to our parents. By 'us' I mean my generation, people born after the Change. You know that thing where you break up with someone and say, It's not you, it's me? This is the opposite. It's not us, it's them. Everyone knows what the problem is. The diagnosis isn't hard – the diagnosis isn't even controversial. It's guilt: mass guilt, generational guilt. The olds feel they irretrievably[1] fucked up the world, then allowed us to be born into it. You know what? It's true. That's exactly what they did. They know it, we know it. Everybody knows it.

To make things worse, the olds didn't do time on the Wall, because there was no Wall, because there had been no Change so the Wall wasn't needed. This means that the single most important and formative[2] experience in the lives of my generation – the big thing we all have in common – is something about which they have exactly no clue. The life advice, the knowing-better, the back-in-our-day wisdom which, according to books and films, was a big part of the whole deal between parents and children, just doesn't work. Want to put me straight[3] about what I'm doing wrong in my life, Grandad? No thanks. Why don't you travel back in time and unfuckup[4] the world and then travel back here and maybe then we can talk.

There are admittedly some people my age who are curious about what things were like before, who like to hear about it, who love the stories and the amazing facts. Put it like this: there are some people my age who have a thing[5] about beaches. They watch movies and TV programmes about beaches, they look at pictures of beaches,

1 irretrievably: *unumkehrbar* **2** formative: *prägend* **3** put sb. straight: tell sb. about his/her mistake(s) **4** unfuckup sth. (infml): make sth. good again
5 have a thing about sth. (infml): like sth., be passionate about sth.

they ask the olds what it was like to go to a beach, what it felt like to lie on sand all day, and what was it like to build a sandcastle and watch the water come in and see the sandcastle fight off the water and then succumb to it, a castle which once looked so big and invulnerable, just melting away, so that when the tide goes out you can't see that there was ever anything there, and what was it like to have a picnic on the beach, didn't sand get in the food, and what was surfing like, what was it like to be carried towards a beach on a wave, with people standing on the beach watching you, and was it really true the water was sometimes warm, even here, even this far north? There are people who love all that shit. Not me. Show me an actual beach, and I'll express some interest in beaches. But you know what? The level of my interest exactly corresponds to the number of existing beaches. And there isn't a single beach left, anywhere in the world.

Not everyone agrees with me on this. Maybe most people don't. Lots of people like to watch old movies where everyone is on the beach all the time. My view? Stupid.

My mother is hard going[1]. She just feels guilty all the time; her expression in repose[2], whenever I'm in the room, resembles a grieving sheep. Just below the surface she's furious too, obviously, because feeling guilty all the time makes people angry, but she channels it into martyrdom[3] and being saintlike and doing everything and never saying a harsh word no matter how badly I screw up[4] and never being angry, just sometimes (and never explicitly) the teensiest[5] bit, you know … disappointed. The time I took their car without permission, got drunk, overrode[6] the autopilot, slid off the road and hit a tree and trashed the battery, which wasn't covered by the insurance because of the whole drunk + underage thing? Not angry, not at all, I'll just go and clean the kitchen and put out your school

1 be hard going: be hard to understand **2** in repose: in a state of relaxation
3 martyrdom [ˈmɑːtədəm]: *Märtyrertum* **4** screw up (infml): make a big mistake
5 teensy (infml): tiny **6** override sth.: *etw. außer Kraft setzen*

uniform for tomorrow, I know you didn't mean to let us down[1] darling and I'm sorry I can't help it if I feel a little bit … sad.

My father is worse than my mother. The thing about Dad is he still has the emotional reflexes of a parent. He wants to be in charge, to know better, to put me straight, to tell me about back in the day[2], to start sentences with the words 'When I was …' He used to do this when I was little, at school, helping me with homework or showing me how to do small practical things. Shoelaces at five, wiring plugs[3] at fourteen, that sort of thing. To be fair, he was pretty good at it. In a different world he'd have been a good father. But it stopped working once I became a teenager and it started to sink in that the world hadn't always been like this and that the people responsible for it ending up like this were our parents – them and their generation. I don't want to know their advice or to know what they think about anything, ever.

So a week at home is as you'd expect. My mother manages to make the task of running the household and feeding three adults seem like the world's most demanding job. We aren't rich enough to have Help – Help is free but you have to feed and clothe and house it so the costs still add up. It's fair enough that there is a lot of work, though we have a washbot and a cleanbot[4] so it maybe isn't quite as much work as all that. Maybe not as much as my mother makes it seem, when I'm at home. Basically, she acts like she's the bravest, keenest, most willing slave in the salt mine. We hardly ever speak, except for her to ask whether I liked it, if there's anything special I'd like for [next meal], do I want to see any of my friends [to which the answer is, why is that any concern of hers?], can she get me anything? Would I like a cup of tea in the morning? It's like staying in a well-run[5] but emotionally suffocating[6] B&B[7].

I'd be lying if I said this brought out the best in me.

1 let sb. down: disappoint sb. **2** back in the day: the old days **3** plug: *Stecker*
4 washbot, cleanbot: washing robot, cleaning robot **5** well-run: well-managed
6 suffocate sb.: kill sb. by depriving him/her of oxygen **7** B&B: Bed and Breakfast, simple hotel

As for my father, he's at work in the day at his office, and then home in the evening to eat whatever my mother has cooked and then watch television/movies/whatever. We don't talk much and both prefer it that way.

All of this was completely as usual; in the words of the song, same as it ever was. I tend to go out to see old mates. But there are fewer of them around than usual, because people my age are all off on the Wall and some of them are still on shift, or on training, or at home. The main topic of conversation: being on the Wall. People compare complaints. Our company sounds like one of the strictest there is – some of them only have ten people on watch at a time, so you get one day or night in three off! That's against the rules and if the Others come you're finished, but the thinking is that if the Others come you're finished anyway.

Let's just say, that's not how the Captain sees it. I bitched about my company for a bit and everyone said I was unlucky to be somewhere so hardcore. I agreed and joined in the moaning[1], but I was, secretly, proud to be going through such a strict version of Defending. I was a real Defender. If you had one day in three off, that made you less of a Defender. Two thirds of one. Not that other people could see this distinction between real Defenders (i.e. me) and the others – all they could see was a group of Defenders in the pub, getting drunk. They steered well clear[2]. Even the ones, maybe especially the ones, young enough to have done stints as Defenders themselves were careful to keep a distance. They knew that we knew how little we had to lose. What would anybody do – send us to the Wall? Besides, the courts are notoriously lenient[3] on Defenders. We get in fights, we bust places up[4], and nothing much happens. Quite bloody right.

Talking to my old mates, I came to realise that life was going to be divided into two, before the Wall and after the Wall. It was as if this thing we had in common was coming between us; the Wall

1 moaning (n): complaint **2** steer well clear (of sb.): keep a distance (from sb.)
3 lenient: *nachsichtig* **4** bust sth. up (infml): destroy sth.

was the same for everybody, but it was different for everybody too. Maybe we'd go back to having our lives in common in two years' time (or rather in ninety-eight weeks' time, I'd gone fully over to the Defenders' habit of counting time not by the calendar but by the number of weeks you've put in), but for now, we were friends because of things in the past, not the present. The main lesson I took from my week at home: my Wall company was what I had in my life now, instead of family and friends.

When I left on the return journey, walk bus train another train lorry, I said goodbye to my mother and father at the front door. A shy hug from my mother, and a handshake from my dad. I could see in his eyes that he wanted to say something, dispense[1] some advice, and he could see in mine that I wasn't having it[2]. I picked up my rucksack and started out but when the door closed, I stopped and waited at the window for a few minutes. It was dark out and they couldn't see me. The light in the hallway went off, then the light in the sitting room went on, then the television went on, then they started watching the programme they'd clearly been waiting a whole week to watch. I don't know whether it was a documentary or a film, I didn't wait to see, but the opening shots showed sand and blue sky and deeper blue water, and small figures climbing up onto boards and riding waves and falling off into the water. My parents had waited for me to leave and then turned on a programme about surfing.

1 dispense sth. (fml): give sth. **2** not have it (infml): *nichts davon wissen wollen*

8

Then it was back to the Wall. The second cycle was harder because our squad switched over and were on the night shift. I had thought the twelve hours of day watch was difficult, but the nights were worse. The dark makes it harder, obviously. The type 2 cold, which is much more likely to come at night, makes it harder too – the cold which is like glue, like mud, which makes it so hard to move it's as if the Wall's concrete is still wet. But the real difficulty is because it's easier to be apprehensive at night. That deep, black part of the brain which by day secretly wonders what it would be like if the Others came, and wonders if it would really be so bad, by night is given over to fear.

At night, on the Wall imagination is not your friend. The distracting thoughts which help you get through the day – about being somewhere else, about what you'll do when you get off the Wall, about food, about sex – don't work as well. You see things and hear things that aren't there. You know this, and you train for this, but at the same time you know that sometimes, those things are there, and that many times the following has happened: a Defender who thought for a moment he saw something which looked like moonlight gleaming off metal, and dismissed it, or thought he heard something like metal scratching on concrete, and dismissed it, died coughing up blood with an Other's knife in his guts[1]. You don't get through a twelve-hour shift without having your adrenaline triggered at least once. You tell yourself to calm down, then you tell yourself that there's maybe something there after all. Up down up, like taking pills. You never get used to it, and the best you can hope for is that you get used to not getting used to it.

1 gut (n): intestine, inner organ

We saw much more of the Captain at night. I know it doesn't sound possible that the presence of one man can make a difference to a fear that's as elemental and basic as the kind you get standing guard in the dark against the Others. It did, though. You knew that at some point in your twelve hours, he would be there, appearing either on foot, marching down the ramparts through the pools of illumination, or on a bicycle, which he never did by day, and which always looked slightly incongruous[1]. He was a big man and the bike looked as if it was a size too small for him. Sometimes he would just appear, popping up beside a post without warning, because he had come along the track inside the Wall, the same trick he had used on the first day to catch me daydreaming. (I learned later he did it to everyone on their first day.) He never said much, just stood beside you and looked out at the sea. Then he would make some simple observation, something basic and elemental, about the kind of night it was, dark or less dark, cold or less cold, moonlit or starlit, windy or still, harder to see or less hard, nearly over or just begun. He never told you anything you didn't already know, but it was always just enough to let you know that he had stood on the Wall many times, far more times than you ever would, and he knew it better than anyone, and he was here with you. Then he would nod a farewell, and go on to the next post. Often, in middle stretches on the Wall, halfway between one post and another, he would just stop and stare out at the sea. It was as if he was stretching out his senses, extending the reach of his hearing and vision, out into the dark.

'What do you think the Captain is looking for, when he does that?' I asked Hifa one night. At night we did the same thing we did by day, and met in groups of three for a mid-shift meal. I hadn't realised that you stayed in your pattern of posts for the whole of your two years on the Wall, meaning you ate with the same three people every day, hundreds of times. If you didn't get on with your crew, if they were bullies[2] or idiots or silent or coldly hostile, or just

1 incongruous [ɪnˈkɒŋɡruəs]: strange, not fitting in **2** bully (n, infml): sb. who intimidates and/or harasses others

if the chemistry was wrong, a twelve-hour shift which was already difficult became even more so.

'Maybe he thinks his senses are sharper when there's no one around,' she said. 'You know, the small noises people make. Distractions. Body language. Away from it all. Are you going to finish that?' she asked Shoona, who was making slow progress with that night's energy bar. It had something very sticky in it, maybe dates[1]. In reply Shoona broke it in half and gave the bottom of the bar to Hifa. She took it without saying anything and started eating it. In any other context it would have seemed outlandishly[2] rude, but on the Wall it was a kind of intimacy.

'Four tours ...' said Hifa. 'Imagine doing four tours. Eight years on the Wall.'

'He was a sergeant by the end of his first tour,' said Shoona. 'He just has a knack[3] for it.'

'Yeah, well, imagine having a knack for it,' said Hifa. 'I mean, of all the things you could have a knack for.'

'Juggling[4],' I said.

'Knitting,' said Shoona.

'Sex,' said Hifa.

'Sleep,' I said.

We didn't say much after that.

I finished my food and my hot drink and got up to go back to my post. At night, even the young and the fit stiffened up quickly, and I could feel how the cold had taken up residence in various parts of my body while I was sitting – my hips, my knees. Hifa and Shoona got up too and we split up. I went to the edge of the illuminated ground around my post, about fifty metres away, and jogged back and forwards to the far edge for a few minutes, getting out of breath and warming up but being careful to stop short of sweating. At one end of my circuit[5], looking out to sea, I thought I saw something. A glimmer of light, was my first thought, out to sea. It was unlikely to

1 date (n): *Dattel* **2** outlandish: very strange and unusual **3** have a knack for sth.: have a talent for sth. **4** juggle: *jonglieren* **5** circuit: circular route

be one of ours: the Guard did go out at night, but when they did, they didn't often use lights. I thought I must have been imagining it, but a few minutes later there was another glint[1], and then another.

'I think I can see lights,' I said over the communicator. I felt embarrassed and frightened at the same time – embarrassed in case I was imagining things, frightened in case it was Others. 'Out to sea.'

'How far out?' asked the Captain. Having his voice loudly in my ear without preamble[2] made me jump[3]; normally he didn't use the communicator.

'It's hard to tell, sir. I'm sorry. Not close but closer than the horizon. Maybe a kilometre or more.'

'How many?'

'Two or three. Winking[4] on and off.'

'OK. Good spot. Keep watching. Don't worry, it happens sometimes.'

'Why?' I asked. 'Sir. What's happening?'

'We don't know,' said the Captain, not in his usual tone of command or rebuke, but as if he was asking the same question. 'It's just something they sometimes do.'

I didn't need to ask who he meant by 'they'. The lights were Others. That was my first encounter with them. Not a face-to-face encounter, because that would involve either them or me dying. But an encounter nonetheless. The first time I saw them. I think that was also the first time I could imagine what it would be like to be an Other, floating in the dark, on some makeshift[5] boat or raft[6] or inflatable[7], staring at the shoreline, looking at the Wall, at the sprinkling of lights above and the steep black dark below. You would be bobbing up and down with the sea swell. You would hardly be able to remember the last time you were warm or dry or safe. We were cold but the Others were colder. We were bored and tired and

1 glint (n): shimmer, faint light **2** preamble: introduction **3** jump: make a quick movement because sth. surprised you **4** wink (v): (here) turn a light on and off quickly **5** makeshift: provisional **6** raft: *Floß* **7** inflatable (n): *Schlauchboot*

uncomfortable and anxious, they were angry and frightened and exhausted and desperate. God, the Wall must look like a terrible thing from the sea, a flat malevolent[1] line like a scar. So blank, so remorseless[2], so implacable. We were used to feeling frightened of them, hostile to them: if they came here, we would kill them. It was that simple. But – how we must seem to them! We must seem more like devils than human beings. Spirits, embodied essences, of pure malignity[3]. If we would kill them on sight, what would they do to us, if they could?

I remember thinking: we don't owe them anything. I'm glad I'm one of us and not one of them. Twenty-six hours later, my second shift ended.

1 malevolent: with the urge to harm other people **2** remorseless: cruel and without mercy **3** malignity [məˈlɪgnəti]: *Boshaftigkeit*

9

It was late afternoon and we were standing near the top of a valley in the Lake District. Our rucksacks sat on the ground next to us. The early part of the day had been cloudy, but the sky cleared and the day was now close to perfect: not too warm when we were walking, not too cold when we were still. The light was almost yellow, not fading yet but beginning to think about it, in that ideal moment when it's like an invisible coating[1] of butter, making everything richer, deeper, more intimate. The hills seemed friendly. I took a drink of water and looked around the mountains and felt glad to be there.

Our next few turns on the Wall had been uneventful. We guarded the Wall, the Captain prowled[2] and scowled[3], Sarge and Yos kept us in order. The days were longer, the nights shorter. The weather warmed up a little. The type 2 cold had largely passed – though when it did come, it was more dangerous than ever, because you could be taken by surprise. One member of our squad, a quiet tall woman who had done a year at college and was about to go back, came to the end of her tour and we gave a party for her. Because we were still on the Wall, it was a sober party, but it was a happy occasion for all that, and it did make me think that time was going past. I was getting through my shifts. Every day that went past, every hour, was bringing me closer to getting away, getting off the Wall, starting the rest of my life. Between those two-week cycles we went 'home' to our families and then did a week on standby duty[4], which was physically much easier than either Wall shifts or training, but was so uneventful it brought other challenges. The next holiday, a group of us decided, we would spend together. So that is what this was: a holiday week with my new friends. I wouldn't have done it if Hifa

1 coating: thin layer covering a surface **2** prowl (v): move quietly like a hunter
3 scowl (v): look at sb./sth. angrily **4** on standby duty: *auf Rufbereitschaft*

hadn't been going, but once she had mentioned it, I latched[1] on to the idea.

None of us had any money, so we thought we'd go camping. We wanted to go somewhere with no view of the sea; with attractive landscape; with nice pubs; with good walking but not too strenuous[2], or only strenuous for those of us who felt like it. Three men and three women: me and Cooper and Hughes, Hifa and Shoona and Mary. Two tents borrowed from the quartermaster[3]. We agreed to leave our communicators behind – a radical move, actually, the first time we'd tried anything of the kind. I hadn't spent a week away from my phone since I first got one at the age of ten. Nature! That was the idea. I'm not saying it was a good idea, just that it was the idea.

Cooper researched the ideal camping spot, just along the hillside from a locally famous pub, but this was our first day, and it wasn't where he had thought it would be. The result was that we were standing here as the day gave signs of ending, no tents pitched[4]. This was a beautiful spot but not necessarily a great campsite.

'Let's go over the hill and see if there's somewhere better,' said Cooper.

'Oh come on,' said Mary. 'I'm knackered[5]. I want my dinner.'

'That pub is out there somewhere,' Cooper said. 'If we had our communicators ...'

'We all agreed,' said Hifa and I together.

'OK, fine, we agreed. And now we're lost.'

'We aren't lost, we just aren't sure where we are. There's a difference,' said Cooper.

'I think I remember this place from when we were talking about it. I think it's just up and over. It could be a kilometre, not much more,' said Shoona. In that mysterious way of group dynamics, her

1 latch on to sth. (infml): become attached to sth. **2** strenuous ['strenjuəs]: requiring a lot of energy and effort **3** quartermaster: army officer responsible for the soldiers' accommodation and clothing **4** pitch (v): (here) put up, erect **5** knackered (infml): extremely tired

opinion decided the matter. Maybe her words carried extra weight because she was more likely to argue with Cooper than to go along with him, so there was no sense of a couple ganging up[1] or siding together. We finished our water, picked up our packs. The Help, who had been standing silently a few metres away, did the same thing.

That was the other big, daring[2], innovative thing we had done for this trip: we had decided to bring Help. We had borrowed them from the ancillary services support section[3] of the Defenders. Help is unaffordable for most ordinary people, but if you're camping, there's no extra food or shelter that the Help isn't carrying for itself, so you basically get the Help for free. It was me who worked this out and me who suggested it and I won't pretend not to be impressed by myself. This meant that instead of carrying exceptionally heavy, unwieldy[4] rucksacks with all our food and gear in them, we were carrying much smaller, lighter, fun-sized holiday packs. We could do whatever we wanted in the day and our campsite would be shipshape[5] when we got back, fire lit, dinner cooking, clothes washed. It would be a taste of what it's like to be rich. I had thought it might be awkward for us, from the human point of view, getting used to Help when we weren't the kind of people who had it in our private lives. But it was interesting how little adjustment it took. The Help were a man and a woman, a couple I think, from their familiarity with each other and the way they hardly spoke. I didn't ask them their story and they didn't offer to tell it, which was perfect too. He did the cooking and she did everything else.

On the first day, Cooper's navigation turned out to be correct. We carried on the track we'd been taking up the hill, the sunlight at our back so the whole landscape looked blessed, flooded with gold. When we got to the top, the view opened out again: a lake stretched out in front of us, with mountains surrounding it on all sides: right in

1 gang up (infml): band together (against the others) **2** daring (adj): willing to take risks **3** ancillary service support section: *Abteilung zur Unterstützung durch Hilfskräfte* **4** unwieldy: big and difficult to move or carry **5** shipshape (infml): tidy and clean

the middle of the lake a paddle boat[1] was puffing out steam. There was a moment like one of those nineteenth-century paintings of a Romantic dude having conquered a peak and surveying the world laid out beneath him, except the painting would have some additional details: six scruffy[2] Defenders, two Help, and also the Defenders were all doing a little celebratory dance because they'd found the pub they were looking for. It was about half a kilometre down the other side of the hill, with a small, perfectly sited campground sharing the same view we'd had from the top.

'Result,' said Cooper, pleased with himself. We left our bags and went into the pub while the Help set up our camp. Yes, I thought – this must be what it's like to be in the elite. To have things done for you. To be on the inside. The pub was an old-time fantasy of an English inn, with saloon and lounge and snug[3], wood panels, cosy: you could imagine arriving here on a winter night and immediately feeling safe and warm. The landlord was, we could tell after about ten seconds, a former Defender who gave special treatment to people doing their time on the Wall. The first set of pints[4] was on the house. We had one more round, then went back out to our tents, where the Help had begun cooking over the campsite fire. It was now dark, but a deep blue moonlit dark, the kind Defenders like. Fire, woodsmoke, mutton: everything was perfect. The Wall felt a very long way off.

The next morning I woke early, not long after first light. I got out of the tent to stretch the sleep out of me and look for coffee. I wasn't wearing my glasses so things were blurry, and I had a sudden hallucination: a figure in white, backlit by the rising sun, slowly dancing, aflame with light. I thought: an archangel! I thought: I'm going mad! I thought: sweet baby Jesus, that's Hughes doing tai chi. He didn't stop or turn to look at me but kept at his practice. It was impressive and also ridiculous – impressive in part because he must have known it looked ridiculous, but that wasn't stopping him or slowing

1 paddle boat: paddle steamer (*Schaufelraddampfer*) **2** scruffy (infml): shabby **3** snug (n, BE): (here) small separate room in a pub **4** pint: unit of measurement (1 pint = 0.568 l); (here) glass of beer

him down. Was he good at it? I think maybe he was. It looked rhythmical enough and he didn't fall over.

The Help wasn't up yet but Hughes had brewed up a pot of coffee on a stove and I took some. I sat on one of the camp stools and looked out at the view. I got on well with Hughes, and the odd thing, apart from the fact that we were physically a little alike, was that he had grown up near me, a town about fifteen miles away. It turned out we knew people who'd been to school with each other. At handover once, Sarge shouted at Hughes for being in the wrong place, then when he saw who it was apologised, or sort-of apologised. His exact words were 'Sorry, got the wrong tall thin streak of piss[1].'

By the time I finished a mug of coffee Hughes had finished doing his exercises.

'Sorry,' he said. 'I know it looks stupid.'

'No ...' I started to say. Then I shrugged. 'Just different. From, you know, fix bayonet, point automatic weapon, pull trigger.'

'I can't do it on the Wall, people would take the mickey[2]. I'd never hear the end of it.'

'Yeah, I can see that.'

'Also you're supposed to do it outdoors and most of the time it's too fucking cold.'

'Yeah, I can see that too.'

'My teacher would say I should just ignore it. The cold and the teasing. I can't, though.'

'What is he, some ninety-year-old Chinese dude with whiskers[3], who's been doing martial arts[4] so long he can, like, fly?'

'No, he's called Graham, about thirty-five, from Wolverhampton. But he does know his tai chi.'

'You planning to go back there?'

1 streak of piss (infml, derog): tall and skinny person **2** take the mickey (out of sb.) (infml): make fun (of sb.) **3** whiskers (pl): *Schnurrbart* **4** martial arts: combat sports such as kung fu and judo

'No. I'm going to go to college.' He reached down into a bag and pulled out a book, a paperback copy of Wordsworth's[1] selected poems. 'I want to study literature. I might stay on at uni and teach if I can make a go of it[2].'

I looked at Hughes. The bulky, looming, whiskery figure I usually met trudging down the Wall in twilight, muttering curses under his breath and glaring[3] at me and carrying an automatic weapon in his right hand rather than slung over his shoulder – that person was a skinny, gentle intellectual who did meditative martial arts and read Romantic poetry and wanted to be an academic.

'You?' he asked.

'I don't know,' I said, and found, to my surprise, that the thought was true. I used to have secret ideas about what I wanted to do: secret in the strong sense that I had never told anyone. I wanted to get away from home (that part was no secret), to get as much education as I could, to get a job where I made lots of money, and to become a member of the elite. All this was too vague to count as a plan. I didn't know anyone who had done it; I didn't know the detail of how to do it; but I knew that it could be done. Elites have to let in some outsiders: that is a basic rule of how they work. It's how they renew themselves and how they spread just enough of the benefits around to stop disorder rising from below. Also: elites need new blood because it's the newly arrived members of the elite who know how the rest of the population are thinking, right now. Not in general terms, but right in this specific historical moment. To find that stuff out, you have to let some of them in. Somebody like me, a bright ambitious provincial boy.

This was secret, dark, private. I knew enough to know that this was not a good thing to want, and not a good way to be: that at the same time I was in the middle of my friends and peers and colleagues, my fellow Defenders, I was privately scheming to get away from them, to become somebody else. I was in effect saying that I

1 William Wordsworth (1790–1850): English Romantic poet **2** make a go of it (infml): make it, be successful **3** glare at sb.: look at sb. aggressively

was better than them – not saying it out loud, but doing something much worse, saying it in my heart. My deepest thought was: I'm not like you. You don't know me.

And yet, to my surprise, I found that this secret idea of mine, about who I really was, seemed to be wearing off[1]. The more time I spent with them, the more I realised I was more like the other Defenders than I was unlike them. At first I looked at those planes flying overhead and I longed, physically ached, to be up there looking down rather than down here looking up. To see the world spread out below, to be up there in the blue, to be so far up above you could no longer see people – that was it. To go up above people, to be away from ordinariness, to live in the pure inhuman element of height and air. I still felt the appeal of that, the thrill of it. To be up there rather than down here ... but the problem was, that was the same as wishing to be above normal people, not one of them. To say, I'm more like those people up in the plane than I'm like Sarge and Yos and Mary and Cooper and Shoona and Hughes and Hifa and even my parents. To be one of them and not one of us. But I was realising that maybe I didn't want to be one of them; maybe I liked us more than I liked them. Though those planes still looked very beautiful, and it must be amazing to be that far up, to be moving that quickly, to be able to look down as you fly ...

'Yeah, I don't know. College. Then, I don't know.'

'No point pretending to know when you really don't.'

'No.'

Mary was the next one up. She came out of the girls' tent yawning and stretching, her curly hair seeming to stretch too, up and out. She came over and helped herself to coffee – she was one of those temperamentally cheerful people who are hilariously[2] moody in the morning until they've had some caffeine. After she finished her cup she was ready to talk.

'I wonder what they're planning to cook tonight,' she said. Although one of the reasons we had Help was so that we didn't have

1 wear off: disappear slowly **2** hilarious: very funny

to cook, cooking was Mary's hobby and chief interest as well as her job: it was just her favourite thing to do. No need to ask her what her plans were for life after the Wall. It was her favourite topic of conversation, a running reverie[1] about what she'd do once she had the money to open her own place. (That part, the bit where she put together the money, was a little vague. But she had faith.) When she could cook whatever she wanted, as long as it was in season. She loved to talk about it.

'The produce you could get before the Change,' she said. 'Everything, all the time. Tomatoes and fruits, hams from you name it, meat whenever you liked, all of it all the year around. Oils, spices, herbs all year round, anything you wanted from anywhere at any time. I read those old books, I think, it must have been too easy, you know? You could just cook anything. Whenever. It just makes you think, how did people know what to want? I mean, if it's anything you like, any time, it's like science fiction, where they have a machine that just makes stuff. It does your head in[2]. Press a button, and it's roast beef, pheasant mole[3], chickpea fritters[4] in yoghurt dressing, aioli[5], prawn[6] curry, mango soufflé[7], duck blood stir fry[8], consommé[9], you know, where does it all end? I mean, the idea is amazing, everything all the time, I get it, and yet, it's weird and wrong too. Now, there's less, but maybe, I don't know, I wouldn't say it's better, that would be mad, obviously it's not better, but you have to work with what you've got, you know, and even if it is, you know, turnips[10], turnips, fucking turnips yet again, at least you know you're working with turnips because that's what came out of the ground and that's what you've got to cook and that's what you've got to make interesting, because there's no choice, you know? And then it's cabbages or celeriac[11] or swedes[12] or beetroot[13] or berries, it is whatever it is that comes out

1 reverie: pleasant daydream **2** do sb.'s head in (infml): confuse sb. **3** mole ['moʊleɪ]: type of sauce **4** fritter: fried food **5** aioli [aɪ'əʊli]: garlic mayonnaise **6** prawn: *Garnele* **7** soufflé ['su:fleɪ]: oven-baked dish made from egg whites, milk and flour **8** stir fry (n): dish with fried pieces of food **9** consommé ['kɒnsəmeɪ]: clear soup **10** turnip: *Steckrübe* **11** celeriac: *Knollensellerie* **12** swede: yellow root vegetable **13** beetroot: root vegetable with dark red colour

of the ground and that's what's amazing and beautiful about it, you know, that's what's interesting, not just going to the shops and being able to buy, you know, stuff that just got off a plane from who knows where.'

She found it hard to leave the Help to get on with it, and spent the first few days hovering[1] over the cook and making suggestions which, to judge from his body language, he didn't entirely appreciate. A proud man, you could see that. And yet by the end of the week they were cooking together, despite Shoona telling her she was an idiot and the whole point of the holiday was not to be doing the very exact same thing she spent all her time doing when she was on the Wall. Mary's reply: 'But I want to.' There's never any answer to that.

Another question pressed on me while we were on holiday. It was: when did Cooper and Shoona have sex? This was a mystery at barracks, and even more so here. We had asked them if they wanted a tent of their own – well, I say we, it was Hifa asking Shoona in private – and they had said no. Fine, but when and where did they do it? It must have involved sneaking off outdoors, or round the back of buildings, or something. They never made any public gestures of affection and were in no obvious sense a couple, except they were.

My own plans in that direction came to nothing. I tried a couple of times to go off for walks with Hifa, but one of the problems with camping, it turned out, was that there was almost no privacy. Every time I made a sneaky suggestion – fancy a trip to the pub? fancy seeing what's over that hill? fancy a walk down to the nearest village? fancy borrowing a couple of rods[2] from the landlord and going to try some fishing? – she would either immediately ask the others if they wanted to come too, or they would see us heading off and join us without asking, as if everyone had automatic permission to join in anything anyone else was doing. I felt pathetic[3], as if I'd gone back to school and wasn't all that far away from the stage of sexual development where boys' way of showing girls that they like them

1 hover over sb.: (here) watch sb. closely, follow sb. closely **2** rod: stick used for fishing **3** pathetic: *jämmerlich, armselig*

is to go up to them and pull their hair and then run to the other end of the room.

I still often think of that week. Maybe that's in part because of what happened afterwards. But at least some of it is because it was a magical seven days. I can't say it was the happiest time I spent on the Wall, because the whole point is that we weren't on the Wall, we were on holiday; but it was the best time I ever spent with my new Wall family. We walked, talked, ate, read. Drank a fair bit but never so that we were too hungover[1] to enjoy the day after. The landlord let us use the bathrooms of the pub; he even let us wash and shower there. We got to know each other differently. Being a Defender was a personality people put on when they went to the Wall. Their non-Wall self was closer to their real self, maybe. Or maybe not, I now think, maybe there isn't a real self, just different versions of us we wear in different settings and with different people. The me who deals with my parents is not the me who talks to Hifa and that is not the me who takes orders from the Captain and that is not the me I am inside myself during a shift on the Wall, counting down the minutes to the end of the twelve hours.

On the last evening I finally managed to get Hifa to go off on her own with me, by sidling[2] up to her, raising my eyebrows and asking, 'Walk?' And just like that we set off down the hill from our camp. We walked down and around a col[3], then up to the top of a long valley and stood looking back down at the view. We were across the far side of the bowl of hills from where we were camping and we could just see the pub. There was a final-night feeling, that back-to-school, back-to-reality vibe which you always get in the moments before you set off home at the end of a successful holiday. I thought: this is my moment to say something. Or maybe, don't say anything, just make my move? Hifa was panting slightly from the exertion[4] of

1 be hungover: have a hangover, suffer from the aftereffects of drinking too much alcohol **2** sidle up to sb.: approach sb. without being noticed **3** col: mountain pass **4** exertion: physical effort

walking the last stretch uphill, her hair pulled back by her knitted cap, her skin flushed, her lips full and pink.

'When I grow up I'm going to be rich enough to have Help,' Hifa said, not forcefully but as if she was daydreaming. And just like that I felt my moment go. She had said something which I'd been thinking, but felt was too private to say. Wanting to have Help was on my secret wish list, or had been, and this experience did nothing to change that. If anything it made it seem more desirable. I had thought that Help was a status symbol, a technique for signalling that you're rich. But the thing I learnt that week was how much nicer life could be if you had somebody else to do all the boring and difficult bits for you. Having Help was like having a life upgrade. I also realised this was one of the differences between me and Hifa. Because she didn't think she'd ever be rich enough to have Help, she felt free to talk about it, disguised as a joke. Because I thought I would one day be rich enough, because my whole sense of myself was that I was going to be the kind of person who was rich enough, I'd never make a joke about it. That would be giving away real information about who I was and what I wanted.

'Time to go back, the sun's about to go down,' she said, turning from the view. I could lunge[1]? No, too late, too desperate. I had missed my chance. I also thought, wow, it's funny how I don't really know anything about you.

The last morning came: back to reality. We packed, and headed off to the train station to make the trip to the Wall. Our packs, which had felt light on the way to the holiday, were heavy as we set out on the return journey. We'd spent the whole week talking and arguing and joshing[2], but we were quiet on the train. I was still brooding[3] on the issue of Help when we said goodbye at the big terminus in London. There was something I'd been thinking about that week. I'd never really thought about Help before, either having it or being it, and the linked question of what their lives had been like before

1 lunge (at sb.) (v): make a sudden movement (towards sb.) **2** josh sb.: tease sb.
3 brood on sth.: think about sth. intensively

and after the Change, and the journeys they had made to get here, and how they had got over the Wall, and what it had been like to be among the Others and now to be Help. I could just about imagine burning sand, a huge yellow sun close overhead, salt water stinging in cuts, the weak being left behind, the bitter tastes of exile and loss, the longing for safety, the incandescent[1] desperation and grief[2] driving you onwards ... no, I couldn't really imagine. And yet here they were.

I don't know why the thing I wanted to know felt like an awkward question, but it did, and I'd been storing up my nerve to ask. At the station, the Help were leaving us to go to their next assignment. As we Defenders had agreed, I took the cook aside for a moment to thank him and slip him an envelope with a tip for him and his partner – you aren't supposed to do that, but we thought it was the right thing. He took it with an inclination of his head. The only time I'd seen him smile, or even change expression, was on the last couple of days of the holiday, when he was cooking with Mary. This was my last chance. The station was busy and crowded, which created a sense of intimacy around our talk: we couldn't be overheard[3].

'I have something I wanted to ask,' I said. The Help was a thin man, economical in movement, and whenever you spoke to him he stayed impassive[4], his hands by his sides. 'What happened to the world, we here have a name for it, we call it the Change. But what I've been wondering is what other people call it, if there's a word for the same thing, or if it's just something that happened. I hope you don't mind me asking, but is there a word for the Change, what we call the Change, in your language?'

'Coo-ee-shee-a,' I thought he said. I didn't know if I'd heard that correctly and had no idea what it meant, but there was something in his eyes that stopped me from asking more. He picked up his bag and he walked off with his partner, not saying goodbye and not looking back.

1 incandescent: full of burning feelings **2** grief: profound sadness **3** overhear sb.: secretly listen in on sb. **4** impassive: indifferent, emotionless

We went to the safe deposit[1] office and picked up the precious cargo we'd left there before heading north: our communicators. Hifa kissed hers before turning it on and said, 'I've missed you so much.'

I wanted to look at my communicator in private. I put it in my pocket and waited until the others had started off for our train back to the Wall. The station was still frantic[2], mainly with commuters rushing home: it was one of those moments when you remember just how much life there is away from yours, away from being a Defender. All these people had homes, pay packets[3], families, hobbies, taxes to pay, things on their mind, TV series to catch up with, heating bills, gardens to plant. I had none of those things; maybe one day I would. At the moment I didn't particularly want them. It was odd: I wanted to get off the Wall, I wanted this time to be over, yet when I tried to think hard about what would be next, there was a blank[4].

I switched on my communicator. There were lots of messages but before I looked at them I went onto the net to look something up: coo-ee-shee-a. I didn't get it right first time because I spelt it wrong, but on the third attempt I found what I was looking for. *Kuishia* is a Swahili word. It means 'the ending'.

1 safe deposit: *Schließfach* **2** frantic: (here) full of people moving in a hurried way **3** pay packet: wage, salary **4** blank (n): empty space

10

When we went back to the Wall it wasn't strictly 'back' but to a new location on the east coast. Remember, two weeks on the Wall, two weeks off, of which the first week is holiday and the second week is (usually) training. This was a training section. Defenders looked forward to these. Basic training was generally felt to be hell – that was the whole point of it, to toughen you up, get you used to all the new norms of the Wall, break you down and build you up again as a Defender. Once you were on the Wall, though, training weeks were, relatively speaking, fun. For a start, every week you spent training was one less week on the Wall. You were in a new place, not your usual watchtower. Also, training meant you were doing new things – no point training at the stuff you can already do.

We were sent to an early section of the Wall on a river estuary[1]. Most of the old riverscapes[2] have gone since the Change – it's another thing we see only in pictures. Here, though, accidents of topography mean it still looks more or less the same as it does in old photos. There are sloping[3] riverbanks, trees overhanging the water, a gentle curve of slow-moving water and greenery. This was one of the very first bits of the Wall to be built, and it was never used. The reason: as the Change progressed, engineers realised that the Wall needed to start further out, so the river mouth was concreted over and the direction of the Wall had been reshaped. The result was a section of the Wall built to the usual specs[4], but not in active use. A perfect spot for training. Also, because this wasn't the Wall proper[5], there was Help. Kit[6]-cleaning and barracks maintenance was done

1 river estuary: place where a river flows into the sea **2** riverscape: river landscape **3** sloping: *geneigt, abfallend* **4** specs (infml): specifications **5** the Wall proper: the Wall as such, the real Wall **6** kit: equipment

by them. Chores[1] and shitwork? Not on this watch! Now that right there was a little holiday in itself. Mary and the rest of her crew were especially jolly[2], because they had nothing to do: the Help did most of the cooking. They just sat around all day watching TV and playing games on their communicators. It would have been more annoying if they hadn't been so openly gleeful[3] about it that they were hard to resent.

'This is a defend–attack exercise,' said the Captain, the morning after we got to the watchtower. We were sitting in the barracks main room, which was the same as our own main room, except here you could see trees through the window – which made it feel very different. 'We have a five-kilometre section of Wall to defend for three days and three nights. Note that that's two K more than our usual distance. We'll be stretched. Each Defender will be guarding three hundred and thirty metres of Wall, not two hundred. Trust me: it's harder. Much harder. The other squad will be attacking at some point over the next three days. Maybe more than once. I don't know anything about them, who they are or where they're from or what their numbers are. I'm guessing they're the same size unit as us, but I don't know that and we can't act on that assumption. We have to treat them exactly the same way we would treat Others. Except,' he gave one of his rare, startling smiles, 'with blanks[4] instead of live ammo. You have a detector on your jacket. If it flashes, you're wounded but can keep fighting, if the light turns solid, you're dead. There are assessors[5] to watch the fight. White armbands. If they tell you you're dead, you're dead. Don't mess with them, they have the power to give you extra time on the Wall. They film the fight with static[6] and head cams too, and the ruling about who's dead and who's got through is made by combining what the assessors say with what they see on the footage[7]. Any questions?'

1 chore [tʃɔː(r)]: boring or unpleasant work **2** jolly (adj): happy **3** gleeful: happy, cheerful **4** blank (n): (here) cartridge that contains no bullet, only explosives **5** assessor: person who judges sb.'s performance **6** static: static camera **7** footage: video material showing a particular event

We shuffled about a bit. Sarge eventually said, 'Tell them about the fun part, sir.'

The Captain actually laughed. It was clear he loved this kind of training – loved being active and doing things, as opposed to waiting for something to happen and being permanently on guard. He was still smiling.

'Yes – the fun part. After our three days we have a day to swap locations with the other squad, and then to make our own plans. Then, we're the attackers.' I noticed he didn't say, we're the Others. I was glad of it. The words would have seemed wrong; would have triggered a superstitious twinge[1]. Nonetheless, it's what he meant, and was obviously what he was most looking forward to. The Captain, who had been an Other, loved the idea of playing at being an Other again, and play-acting at doing the thing he had once done for real.

'We're going to make their lives hell, for three days, and some of us are going to get over the Wall. I've done this exercise a number of times and I've never failed to get some of my squad over, and this time will be no exception. Think about it when you're on duty and we'll discuss and make plans on the turnover day. We're going to get over the Wall. You can all contribute ideas about how to do that. And I,' he smiled again, 'I've got some ideas too.'

The session then became a general briefing about our section of the Wall, the peculiarities of its geography and topography. The headline news was that the riverbanks around here had been high and had descended to the river almost like cliffs, but cliffs which went up in stages, say five metres straight, then a small flat section, then another five metres. The steep banks were why the engineers had at one point thought the Wall could run here without much difficulty. They had turned out to be wrong, but only after they built the Wall. The result was that there was a ledge[2] of riverbank left at the bottom of the Wall, not exactly like one of the old world's beaches, but wide enough to stand and walk on. This made the old cut-off

1 twinge: sudden uneasy feeling **2** ledge: narrow flat area

section of the Wall a very useful place for attackers, since there was somewhere they could perch[1]. It was going to be an interesting week.

I don't think I ever saw our company in a better mood than during those seven days training. It really was like a holiday, or a holiday camp, because there was a structure, the unforgiving structure of shifts, but also the change of location, the extra freedom of having Help, and, crucially, new faces. The Defenders who'd been there longer than I had knew their opposite numbers, their shift twins, but I only really knew Hughes. The rest of the other shift I'd met solely on those drunk, civilian-frightening train journeys at the end of our deployments[2]. It was entertaining to see how closely they paralleled us, with a new one (like me), a funny one, a grumpy one, one who needed to be told everything three times. They even had one whose hobby was whittling, just like Yos.

I was nervous when I started my first turn on the training section of Wall, or fake-Wall. To mix things up we would do three days of nights and three of days with a complicated mixed swing-shift[3] in the middle. Our section started on nights, which was both good and bad, since it meant we were getting the hardest part over straight away, but on the other hand was more of a jolt[4], given that we'd just had a week off. The fact that we were on a not quite real version of the Wall felt strange: I was nervous, while also knowing that deep down there wasn't much reason to be nervous, not really, since this wasn't like really being a Defender and so if I failed to do my job I wasn't going to, you know, die. Also the scenery here was much more interesting, basically because there was some, as opposed to none at all except concreteskywaterwind. Here there was also river, a section of Wall curling round a far bend of river, even trees! Just visible on a clear day beyond the far section of Wall was a low range of green hills. By moonlight on that first night the landscape looked like an exotic work of composition, something a person had

1 perch (v): stay for some time **2** deployment: *Einsatz* **3** swing-shift: *Wechselschicht* **4** jolt (n): shock

put together to show what you could do with blacks and whites and whatever those other moonlit colours are, not greys, but not normal colours and not black/whites either. Dawn is when you can tell a white thread from a black thread, it says in the Quran. But there are still shadow-colour differences before dawn, when there's moonlight. Also, it wasn't as cold as our section of Wall. I don't know if we were lucky with the weather or if it was something to do with there being less wind in this direction, or some other trick of micro-climate. For whatever reason, it was several degrees milder. Add it all together and it was much less hard. Which made it tempting not to be as vigilant[1] as we were supposed to be.

'This is the life,' someone said over the communicator, that first night. I laughed, then after I had, wondered why it was funny. Eventually I realised: because the idea that standing for twelve hours in the dark and bitter cold with an automatic weapon, waiting for someone to attack you, with certain death the price of failure, marks you in such a way that standing for twelve hours in the dark and slightly less cold waiting for someone to pretend to attack you, by comparison, feels like fun.

The first attack came that night, at four in the morning. It was good tactics on the part of the other squad – a bright moonlit night like this would normally be the last you'd choose for an assault. Also, we thought they'd take at least a day to look at the maps, work out the topography, make a plan. What they did, more simply and more effectively, was to cheat. They didn't approach the Wall over the estuary: they just were suddenly there, pouring over it at well-spaced intervals, silently, like ghosts. I had about five seconds of warning – in the form of weapons fire from a kilometre away, where the middle end of our section was overrun. I looked over, just had time to think, Oh shit, and a strange kind of electric shock, not a thought but a physical sensation, like the one you get when you're watching a horror film and something terrible starts to happen –

1 vigilant (adj): attentive, watchful

you feel it in your back, your spine, your belly, but it's a sensation rather than an idea.

But it's true what Defenders say. The expression we use is that 'your training kicks in[1]'. You find you have these new instincts baked into you. I clicked the safety off my A/R[2] and looked back to my own section to scan. About a hundred metres away I saw two of them half over the Wall: one of them had made it but the other had got stuck and the first man was reaching down to pull his partner over. I lit them up, short bursts, the way I'd been trained. The first man looked over to me, then finished pulling his partner over the Wall, then turned to me with his hands in the air. I'd got them both. While I was congratulating myself on that, though, I heard a cracking sound from behind me and the red light on my chest started flashing. Again, training kicked in. I dived to the ground and rolled right towards the concrete bench at my post. Another two attackers had climbed the Wall in the other direction and were coming towards me. With part of my brain I realised that if this was going on all along our section of Wall, it must mean we were in the middle of a full-company attack, and we were outnumbered two to one: their whole company was attacking our half-company squad. With the rest of my brain I was trying to steady myself enough to aim. I got a long burst[3] off, longer than we were supposed to fire in one go. If you shoot too many rounds at once, the muzzle[4] of your gun travels[5], and you veer[6] off the target.

I was – partly by luck and partly by training – in a good position with decent cover, mostly hidden by the bench, while both the attackers were out in the open. They should have split up and rushed me. Maybe they froze, maybe they thought they'd got me when they came up on me from behind. Mistake. After I got off a long clip[7] one of them raised his hands to put his gun down. The

1 kick in: begin to take effect **2** A/R: automatic rifle **3** burst (n): (here) series of shots **4** muzzle (n): open end of a pistol or rifle **5** travel: (here) be unsteady **6** veer off: not hit **7** clip: (here) small metal container holding several bullets that are shot off one after the other

other, whose red light was blinking, jumped up and began running towards me, jinking[1] from side to side. He was about forty metres away and closing rapidly. I was out of ammo and had to change the magazine, and was grateful for the time Sarge had caught me and bollocked me about taping them together the right way, because I had the new clip in before the attacker got to me and was raising the gun to shoot when the light on my chest went red just as I heard shots from behind me. I couldn't believe it – but no doubt that's what it's like, in a real fight. When you get shot your first thought is that you can't believe it. Ooh I've been shot. Ooh so this is what it's like to be shot. Ooh this is what it's like to be dying, dying, dead ...

Some philosopher said that death is not an event in life. Maybe. It doesn't feel like that in a fight. It feels very much the opposite: that death, yours or your opponent's, is not just an event in life, but the entire point of life. The culmination and meaning of the journey.

I turned. Two of the attackers had come up behind me. A white-armband assessor was with them. I was officially dead. An eerie[2] feeling, or mixture of feelings. I was annoyed, in the way you're annoyed when you're playing a game, and think you're winning, but suddenly lose; I was a little proud, because I'd 'killed' three of them and it had taken six of them to 'kill' me, though it was that irritating kind of pride that you can't express without sounding as if you're boasting, and I knew without having to think about it that boasting about an event which had ended with me being 'killed' would quickly lead to teasing and to a new nickname like, I don't know, Dead Boy; I was a tiny bit relieved, because the fight was over, the tiring bit of the shift was over, the worst had happened, I was done for the night.

The two attackers who had snuck up behind me now put their heads together with the one I'd been shooting at, and began debating what to do next: declare that they had got over the Wall and stop, or run to the next section, several hundred metres away, and join in the ongoing fight there. There was gunfire, but it was spo-

1 jink: change directions while running **2** eerie: strange and scary

radic; it was hard to tell what was going on. I went over to the three 'dead' attackers, who were standing together. It was a rule of these exercises that the 'dead' couldn't talk to the living, but there was no rule to say we couldn't talk to each other.

'Hi,' said one. He broke a piece of chocolate off a bar and gave it to me. Chocolate was a real Defenders' luxury, very hard to get if you were off the Wall, so this was an insider's gesture, a peace offering.

'Thanks. Didn't see that one coming. You were hiding, yeah?'

I'd worked it out: the only way they could have done what they had done was if they'd been concealed on the ledge below the Wall and were waiting for us when we came on shift. Cheating, in other words, since they could never have made it to that spot any other way on a clear moonlit night. My section of the Wall had been swarmed[1]: I found out later that thirty of them, arranged in five groups of six, had attacked five sections of Wall, and mine was one of them.

'Yup.'

'Well, if the assessors let you do it, it's legit[2].'

'Yeah, that's what our Captain said.'

'Done this before?'

'Attack–defend? No. You?'

'No. More fun than being on the Wall, I reckon.'

'No shit.'

The two heroes who had shot me in the back had ended their colloquy[3] and decided to go 'over the Wall', so the fight was officially over. The assessor told the wounded man he wasn't fit enough to go with them, so he started jogging down the ramparts towards the fight in the near distance. The assessor went with him. The attackers and I turned and went off in the other direction, back towards the watchtower and the barracks. One of the men stepped forwards to

1 be swarmed: be overrun by a large group of people **2** legit (infml) [lɪˈdʒɪt]: legal, in accordance with the rules **3** colloquy: conversation

shake my hand. I returned the gesture to the other, who turned out to be a woman. We all seemed somehow to be chums[1].

'Where are you lot staying?' I asked.

'Two barracks along. Just round the river bend so you lot can't see us.'

'How are you getting back?'

'Lorry. At the end of the exercise. Should be there any minute now.'

They gave me another piece of chocolate. About halfway back to the watchtower, I saw Hughes coming towards me. Of course: the Wall never goes unguarded. This exercise was meant to be realistic, so if the Wall had been breached, the new watch would have to come on. As he came closer it was clear that he was too tired to be angry about being woken in the middle of the night.

'Sorry mate,' I said as we passed each other.

'Got any food? We were sent straight out, no time.'

I emptied my pockets. Hughes took what I had. The assessors would have said this was against the rules, but there were no assessors there, so what the hell.

'You kill all this lot?' he asked.

'Three of them. The other two got me.'

'No hard feelings,' said one of the men I'd 'killed', smiling, his voice claggy[2] from the chocolate he was eating. We carried on back to the watchtower. Their lorry was waiting, and we all shook hands again. 'See you later,' I said, which got a laugh, because if I did, it would likely be with me having swarmed over the Wall, and them lying in wait for me, another fight to the 'death'. No hard feelings, the living and the dead, more in common than you might think; a tiny bit of luck here and there dividing them; taking turns to live, taking turns to die; all in the same boat. All the same really. Others, Defenders – what's the difference? I couldn't decide if this was the opposite of what it would be like to fight to the death, or a good preparation for it.

1 chum (infml): friend **2** claggy: *belegt*

11

At the debriefing[1], I thought the Captain would give us a giant bollocking, but that didn't happen. It turned out he'd been in on[2] it all along. That explained why he hadn't been there the night before, which I have to admit I had been wondering about. The two Captains had discussed this sneak[3] attack and ours had agreed to allow the set-up[4]. It was a way of testing our combat skills: not how well we'd catch Others sneaking up on the Wall, but how well we'd do in an all-out fight with a big group who'd got over and ambushed[5] us.

'Not fair? You're probably thinking that. No, not fair. That's the point of the exercise. We train hard to fight easy. This may save your life one day. If you are overrun, you won't be wondering how or why it happened. You'll be fighting for your life. Lessons learned today may save you. Any questions?'

Hifa put her hand up. I was surprised: in groups she was usually quiet. 'Yes. Do we get to do it to them?'

The Captain smiled slowly. 'Oh yeah.'

'Good.'

Thirty of them had attacked. The whole squad, as I'd thought. Eighteen of them had been killed, and seven wounded sufficiently seriously that, according to the assessors, they wouldn't have been able to get away. Five of them had got over the Wall and 'escaped'. In real life, if they really were Others, they wouldn't get far, of course: they didn't have chips. They'd last a few days at best. After being rounded up[6] they'd presumably decide to be Help.

1 debriefing (n): meeting after a mission or an operation to discuss the course of events and people's performance **2** be in on sth. (infml): know about sth.
3 sneak (adj): without warning **4** set-up (infml): (here) deception, trap
5 ambush sb.: attack sb. by surprise **6** round up sb.: find and arrest sb.

Seven of us had been 'killed', all five of the Defenders on the sections which were swarmed, and two others who went to help them. Five wounded. Out of fifteen on our shift, only three of us were 'unharmed'. In real life, if a breach[1] like that had happened, everyone responsible would be put to sea. A Defenders' court would determine how many people that was. For a breach of this scale that could be the entire squad. If the other squad, the day shift, were found to have been slow in reacting, and that had contributed to the breach, some of them would be put to sea too. The Captain went into detail about the attack and our response to it, what had gone right, what had gone wrong. The take-away[2] was clear: if Others get onto the Wall in numbers, and you aren't waiting for them, you're screwed[3].

Hifa had been one of those 'killed'. Her section of the Wall had been swarmed. Whereas I was, I found, pretty chill[4] about being killed – as the Captain said, it was a set-up, the whole point of exercises was that you went through experiences like this – Hifa didn't feel like that. Being riddled[5] with blank automatic bullets had got to[6] her. She was silent and had gone into herself. After the debrief we went and sat in the mess and Help brought us a cup of tea.

'It's fake,' I said to her afterwards. 'It's children playing let's pretend. Think of it as being like a video game.'

'I don't play video games,' she said, which was true. We sat there for a bit. 'Let's pretend ...' she said. 'I used to like that. Let's pretend ... Grown-ups don't do enough let's pretend.'

'You're a grown-up?'

She chucked[7] a peppermint at me. That meant she was feeling better.

'Anyway, this was a nasty version of let's pretend. We're never going to get thirty Others hiding at the bottom of the Wall waiting

1 breach (n): (here) act of breaking through the defense **2** take-away (infml): (here) most important message that people are supposed to remember
3 screwed (infml): lost in a terrible situation **4** chill (adj, infml): cool, relaxed
5 riddled: having a lot of holes **6** get to sb. (infml): affect sb. negatively
7 chuck sth.: throw sth.

when we come on shift. It's as much let's pretend as building a blanket fort[1] and saying it's a castle.'

'What kind of castle?'

'One with pointy turrets[2].'

'Who lives in the castle?'

'A happy ogre[3].'

'Oh! On his own?'

'Not necessarily.'

'A lot of space. Even for an ogre.'

'He needs space.'

'He has commitment issues[4].'

'And his breath is toxic. Literally – it poisons people. Even other ogres.'

'Sounds a bit like Yos.'

'Now that's harsh,' I said.

'I bet the ogre whittles.'

'He can't, his hands are too big, he wants to whittle but he just busts things.'

'Poor ogre.'

'Then he takes the broken pieces of wood and assembles them into sculptures which he sells for enormous amounts of money to collectors. That's how he can afford the castle. But he would trade it all for being able to whittle.'

'I feel sorry for the ogre now.'

'I think you're right to.'

'What does he eat?'

I thought for a moment.

'Children.'

Hifa had a very appealing laugh, half an octave deeper than her speaking voice.

1 blanket fort: castle made by children using pillows and blankets **2** turret: small tower of a castle **3** ogre [ˈəʊɡə(r)]: giant who eats people (in fairy tales) **4** commitment issues: *Bindungsängste*

Sarge appeared at the far end of the barracks. 'Oi! You're back on shift in thirty minutes.' The attack had meant that all the shifts were muddled[1], and we had swapped with the day watch. I sighed, Hifa sighed, we both began to get up and get ready. Sarge was in a good mood because he was one of the people who'd survived the attack (mainly by accident of place, if you ask me, though I wouldn't say that to his face).

We got through the rest of our defensive turn on the pretend-Wall, five more days, without being breached again. That's not the same as saying it was uneventful, because the longest spell between attacks was eighteen hours. Respect to that other company, they really gave it a go[2]. But none of them got over the Wall. To be honest, none of them even got particularly close. A sequence of moonlit nights helped. The estuary landscape meant you didn't have the distant blurred horizons of sky–sea which at dawn and dusk could make the light so difficult. Also, the waves were small to non-existent, river waves, and there was nothing like the chop and roll[3] which would make it so hard at our usual post. So there were factors which helped. Despite that, it was reassuring, after the trauma of that first night, that well-trained attackers coming at you under normal conditions were relatively easy to track and kill. We would see them a few hundred metres off and light them up. The assessors claimed that a few of us were shot by people sniping[4] from boats, but we all thought that was bullshit. Others with snipers using automatic weapons from boats? Sure, and they also ride in seven abreast[5] on trained narwhals[6], blaring[7] Wagner over loudspeakers. Their best attack was on the penultimate night. I slept through it. They swam in a kilometre and tried to climb the Wall solo. The crew on duty let them get close, then picked them off one at a time.

1 muddle sth.: put sth. in the wrong order **2** give sth. a go (infml): try sth. **3** chop and roll: heavy movement of waves **4** snipe (v): shoot at sb. from a hiding place **5** abreast: next to each other **6** narwhal: small whale **7** blare sth. (v): play sth. (music) very loudly

Then it was our turn. We sorted out our stuff, got on a lorry and drove off to the other barracks, which, as the guys from their company had said, was around the corner of the river, two watchtowers away. Halfway there we passed their lorry heading in the other direction, and some pleasantries[1] were exchanged: our entire company stood up and gave them the finger[2], in formation.

The other barracks was the same as every other barracks, except with a few more recreational amenities[3]: table tennis, pool tables, and it even had a gym and a cinema. Of course! The defensive watch had to be on duty all the time, every day, but as attackers, we could pick and choose. We didn't have to work shifts, we could do whatever we liked, schedule-wise. Well, not quite: we'd do exactly what the Captain told us to do, exactly when he told us to do it. Still, by comparison, where the other shift had been a bit like a holiday, this really was a holiday.

The Captain, it goes without saying, had other ideas. We were given orders an hour after we got to the new site. The meeting was held in the briefing room. He was standing next to Sarge and Yos and I wouldn't say he was rubbing his hands with eager anticipation while cackling with glee, because he just wasn't that person, but he was pretty close.

'The fun part!' he said. 'Now, first, a little exercise. Hands up everybody who enjoyed the experience of being overrun by Others, killed and wounded, or surviving only to be put to sea?'

The contrast between what he was saying – naming everyone in the room's worst fear – and his super-jaunty[4] tone was like a slap[5]. Nobody's hand went up.

'Didn't think so,' he said. 'It includes me, by the way. The officer in charge of a company which allows a breach is automatically put to sea.'

1 pleasantry: polite remark **2** give sb. the finger (infml): *jdm. den Stinkefinger zeigen* **3** amenity: sth. that makes a place comfortable **4** super-jaunty (infml): very cheerful **5** slap (n): action of hitting sb./sth. with your hand

I looked around the room. It was clear that most people had forgotten that.

'The reason this is the fun part is, we get to do to them what they did to us. They get to feel what it's like. You're probably wondering how, given that the landscape round here makes the Wall unrealistically easy to defend. They got to ambush us. That was an advantage agreed in advance. In return, we get an advantage, like them, once and once only. A five-minute power cut.'

A shifting and sitting-up took place in the room.

'That's right. Total loss of power for five minutes and five minutes only, on a night of our choosing. The idea is that Others or their sympathisers have co-ordinated a spot of sabotage. You might say it's unlikely, but so was that ambush attack on the first night unlikely. In case you're wondering, that is the standard training exercise here. These two respective advantages are always given to the two companies training on this site. This is our chance to even the score. Except, I don't want to even the score. They got five over the Wall. I want to go not one better, not two better, but twenty-five better. I want to get an entire squad over the Wall. That would be a record and it's a record I want.'

He looked around as if trying to catch someone, anyone, in the act of not wanting the record as much as he did. No takers.

'So how do we do it? I have my ideas. I want to hear yours.'

Silence. Shuffling. More silence.

'This is going to be a very long meeting if nobody has anything to contribute.'

Cooper put his hand up.

'We make it hard for them.'

'Yes, good. How?'

Fidgeting. I think it wasn't so much that people were clueless as that we didn't want to say stupid things in front of the Captain. He had that effect.

Eventually somebody said, 'Keep them on the go.'

'Yes!' said the Captain, almost bouncing. 'Exactly. Keep them at work. Especially at night. All night, every night. Constant attacks.

Some small, some less so. One after another. Make it so that it never stops. Make them tired. And then – the big one.'

So that's what we did. We made a token attack[1] on the second day but apart from that it was just night work. We split into two shifts, again, but with the welcome difference that we were only on for a few hours each; three or four attacks for the first two nights, both shifts taking turns, sleeping as much of the day as we wanted. It was, as the Captain had said it would be, fun. Getting soaking wet and consequently freezing wasn't pleasant, of course, but the basic pattern of being active and on the attack was inherently interesting and involving; knowing what you were doing and when made attacking much less anxious than being a Defender. On the first night our shift even managed to attack twice, catching the waiting lorry back to our barracks, changing into wetsuits and being driven back in motorboats for a second go. (Boat in close, swim in using snorkels.) We all got 'killed', but so what? I understood why the people we'd 'shot' and been shot by in the big assault were in such good humour. I spent more time with Hifa than I ever had before while on duty. I had got to the stage of finding reasons for doing things with or next to her, and was beginning to suspect she was at the same stage too – those little hints you get at the start of something.

Then the last night came, the time for the big assault. In all the time I knew him, I never saw the Captain in a better mood than he was that day. It had all been prep[2] for this: small attacks mainly at the narrow point of the estuary, to misdirect from a single huge attack from the other direction. We had three fast inflatable boats, piloted by members of the Guard. (Not really cheating to use expert pilots: the Others were good sailors, by definition. Any who weren't would have drowned before they got here.) We were favoured by the conditions, moonless and windy. We'd creep in as close as we could, five hundred metres by the Captain's estimate, and on the exact moment of the power cut, the Guard would hit the accelerators and we'd race in. That would take ninety seconds. Focus on three attack

1 token attack: pseudo-attack **2** prep (infml): preparation

points, one for every boat. We had grappling equipment[1] and ladders and the Wall had that attacker-friendly ledge. Sixty seconds to get up and over. Then two and a half minutes of dark to kill as many Defenders as possible and get away from the Wall on the inner side. Our eyes would be dark-adapted; the Defenders' wouldn't be. They'd hear the boats coming but not be able to see them. They'd be knackered from constant attacks all night for the previous sixty hours, and with luck they'd be thinking the end was in sight and the worst over. Our odds were as good as they could be.

I was sitting next to Hughes during the briefing. The Captain was drawing a diagram of fire patterns once we'd got onto the Wall.

'The Captain's good at this, isn't he?' he whispered.

'You'd almost think he used to be an Other,' I whispered back, and immediately felt bad. That wasn't a thing we joked about; it went too deep. What the Captain had lived through before he got here, what he had seen and done, were subjects you felt in his being, rather than topics for gossip. Having said that, when you saw him designing an attack like this, it was possible to understand how he had got over the Wall.

It went more or less exactly as planned. That's rare for anything military. At the debrief, we all agreed the weather had been a big help. The night really was black. There was so much wind the inflatables had to stop further away than we had intended, because the choppy wind-whipped wavelets were pushing us towards the shore. Somebody dropped a rifle against something metal, one of the boat fittings[2], and it felt as if the noise would carry for ten kilometres, let alone the few hundred metres to the Defenders waiting on the Wall. It didn't, though, or if it did nobody noticed. We counted down, looking at our watches, and the lights cut exactly when they were supposed to; the Guards floored it, or hit it, or whatever the verb is for maximum acceleration in a boat. That feeling, the light boat

1 grappling equipment: climbing equipment **2** fitting (n): piece of metal fastened to a boat that holds ropes, rudders, pieces of equipment, etc.

sprinting and bouncing through the total dark, spray[1] all over us, one hand on the rope handrail, the other grabbing our guns, was as pure a feeling of exhilaration as I've ever had.

Splash the last couple of feet. Grapple for security, ladder in place, swarm up, start shooting. The expression 'they didn't know what hit them' is exactly wrong: they knew perfectly well. It's just that they couldn't do anything to stop it. We were ready, we could see, they weren't and couldn't. It was almost unfair, though still not as unfair as the advantage they'd had on the first night. We hit the two Defenders nearest our breach, then eight of our shift got over the Wall and started to get away. I'd agreed to stay and set up a rearguard[2], and so had Shoona. (In real combat I wouldn't have volunteered, I hope it goes without saying. The soldier's most fundamental rule, never volunteer. But on this exercise I thought staying behind and shooting would be more fun.) They got a counter-attack going with about thirty seconds of darkness to spare. Shoona and I got a few of them, then as the lights came on, we went over and slid down the inner side of the Wall. The Defenders shot at us; according to the assessors, afterwards, Shoona got away but I didn't. So what? Our shift alone got eight people over. The others got eleven between them. Nineteen over the Wall was an all-time record. The next best was fourteen. From the moment the lights went out to the moment the assessors said the fight was over was seven minutes. Combat is like that, an undanceable rhythm: slow, slow, slower, sudden pandemonium[3].

When we got back to barracks, the Captain, unlike the rest of us, wasn't elated[4]. He just went calmly round and shook everyone's hand individually, the only time he ever did.

1 spray (n): small drops of water **2** rearguard: soldiers who protect the back part of their troop **3** pandemonium [ˌpændəˈməʊniəm]: chaos **4** elated: very happy

12

The other squad came over and we had a few drinks. No alcohol on the Wall, but this wasn't the real Wall. Somebody put some music on and there was dancing. There was karaoke, and people took turns[1], then one of their squad, a woman, had such an amazing voice we stopped taking turns and listened to her sing soul classics for a while. Then a few more drinks. And a few more after that. Like I said, a holiday. Their squad was supposed to go home to their barracks but it emerged[2] that their lorry drivers had got into conversation with our lorry drivers, and had opened some cans, and then further cans, etc., and they had ended up as hammered[3] as everyone else so there was nobody sober to drive the lorries. They ended up crashing[4] in our barracks, using spare beds, sofas, chairs, even the pool tables. Only a drunk Defender can think a pool table makes an adequate bed.

The next morning we were due to go back to our real posts. That would involve about five hours in the lorry, ash-mouthed[5], suet[6]-faced, smelling of recent disinterment[7]. The other squad had it even worse: they were going back to north Wales. Hifa, who I'd last seen dancing with the woman with the amazing voice, was wearing a beanie, the same one she'd worn in her indeterminate-sex phase[8] when I first met her, and her small features were peeking out from beneath it, scowling with hangover. If I'd been less hungover myself it would have been funny. My day began with an increasingly panicky fifteen-minute search for my glasses, which ended when I realised I'd never taken them off. Before our journey of horror, in the briefing

1 take turns: *sich abwechseln* **2** emerge: (here) come out, become known
3 hammered (infml): very drunk **4** crash (infml): sleep, spend the night
5 ash-mouthed: with a very dry mouth **6** suet: *Talg* **7** disinterment: act of digging up a dead body **8** indeterminate-sex phase: phase in which Kavanagh could not tell whether Hifa was male or female

room, a lecture. Or rather a 'little talk' from a member of the elite, some politician or government official, a short shiny young man with a mop[1] of blond hair in an also shiny suit. He came into the overlit room and stood at the podium. We stand up for officers, but he wasn't an officer, so we stayed put. He looked a little surprised at the state of us. Sixty dishevelled[2] and severely hungover Defenders, unimpressed and unimpressive: not the world's easiest audience.

'Well done!' he said, brightly. They always start by praising you. 'The world's best home defence force, participating in the world's best training programme!'

Both parts of that were news to us, but whatever.

'I've been hearing from your commanding officers. Remarkable!'

I looked across at Hifa, who was sitting next to me. At this close range[3] I could see she was very slightly swaying[4]. Her eyes weren't closed, but on the other hand they weren't fully open either. I gave her a nudge[5], which was a mistake, because she turned towards me and exhaled. Not only could I smell the alcohol, I could actually tell that she'd been drinking spiced[6] rum. Her eyes were bloodshot, which didn't stop her rolling them at the politician.

'We can truly say, this country has never been better Defended. And it is thanks to women and men such as you. I think you deserve a round of applause!'

He began to clap. I think the idea was that we would join in and start applauding ourselves too – yeah! go us! – but he had severely misread the room. We sat there waiting for the point of this, assuming it had a point. It was hard to imagine he'd done this often before. He was a baby politician, an infant member of the elite. He still had his training wheels[7]. I may have been sleep-deprived[8], I might possibly still have been a bit drunk, but I fell for a moment into a reverie, a kind of guided dream, in which I imagined baby members of the

1 mop (n): a lot of thick hair **2** dishevelled: untidy **3** range (n): distance **4** sway (v): slowly move from side to side **5** nudge (n): gentle push **6** spiced: with added flavour **7** training wheels: two extra wheels on a child's bicycle that protect it from falling over **8** sleep-deprived: with a lack of sleep

elite being born from chrysalises[1], already wearing their shiny suits, their ties pre-knotted, their first clichés already on their lips, being wiped down of cocoon matter and pushed towards a podium, ready to make their first speech, spout[2] their first platitude[3], lose their virginity at lying. They'd be made to do that before they were given any food or drink or comfort, just to make sure it was the thing they knew first and best, the thing which came most naturally. They tell us that everyone goes to the Wall, no exceptions. Somehow, though, when I saw the politician, I knew for the first time that that couldn't be true. This man had clearly never been on the Wall. He had never been a Defender. You could smell it on him. It was sometimes said that rich people rigged[4] ID chips so that Help went to the Wall instead of them. You heard rumours about medical exemptions[5], exemptions for extra education. No one ever admitted to not going on the Wall, but we all suspected that there were rich and powerful people who got out of it.

He stopped clapping. You could tell that he could tell that this was going badly, and also that he knew he mustn't show that he knew it. His manner changed and became more brisk[6]. He let some of his sense of his own power show.

'Unfortunately, being a Defender isn't all a matter of praise and compliments. However deserved they might be! And we have some new intelligence[7]. Information with a direct bearing[8] on your –' and it was very interesting the way he said this next word, because you caught a glimpse[9] of something cold and dark in him, just for that tiny moment, a small window into what he really thought of us, and the distance between his life and ours – 'duties.' Our duties. Yes, OK, our duties, our long nights in the cold and dark, twelve hours at a

1 chrysalis [ˈkrɪsəlɪs]: cocoon (of an insect) **2** spout (v): speak in a boring way **3** platitude: statement that everybody has heard before and that is not interesting **4** rig sth. (v): manipulate sth. **5** exemption: official permission to not have to do sth. **6** brisk: energetic, quick **7** intelligence: (here) information gathered by secret agents and spies **8** bearing (n): impact, influence **9** glimpse (n): quick look

time spent both bored shitless[1] and in fear of our lives. That was what, in his eyes, we were for. That was our use, our purpose.

'As you all know, the Change was not a single solitary event. We speak of it in that manner because here we experienced one particular shift, of sea level and weather, over a period of years it is true, but it felt then and when we look back on it today still feels like an incident that happened, a defined moment in time with a before and an after. There was our parents' world, and now there is our world.'

That was sly[2] of him. He was close to us in age, close enough to know how sensitive and how universal this feeling was, about the gulf[3] between us and the generation before. The energy in the room changed. He might be every bad thing we knew him to be but he also knew some truths.

'The Change – before and after. Elsewhere, though, it was not like that. The Change was not an event but a process, a process that in some places, some unlucky places, has not stopped. In many of the hotter places of the world, in particular, the Change is still continuing, still reshaping landscapes, still impacting people's lives. Men and women fled from it, fled from its consequences, tried to make new lives for themselves, to scramble[4] for new shelter, to climb to higher ground, to find a ledge, a cave, a well[5], an oasis, a place where they could find safety for them and their families. But,' he said, his tone changing again, and now he really did sound like a member of the elite, a man used to giving orders and breaking bad news[6], 'the Change did not stop. The shelter blew away, the waters rose to the higher ground, the ground baked, the crops died, the ledge crumbled, the well dried up. The safety was an illusion. So the unfortunates must flee again, and they have begun, again, in numbers, like the numbers from many years ago when the Change first struck. Big

1 bored shitless (infml): extremely bored **2** sly: clever **3** gulf: *Abgrund, Kluft*
4 scramble for sth. (v): fight with others in order to get sth. **5** well (n): hole in the ground from which people can take water **6** break the news: bring the news (in a tactful, considerate way to ease the shock)

numbers, dangerous numbers. So that is the first thing I am here to tell you. The Others are coming. We have had years of relative peace and calm, but that time is now over. You will be busy. The things for which you have been training: you are likely, more likely than for some years, to do them for real.'

Now this really did count as news. I suddenly felt a lot less drunk. Hifa was sitting up straight staring at the man. The rest of the squads were too. Whatever we had thought we were going to hear, it wasn't this.

'The Flight and our friends abroad have confirmed this. Others are on their way. That is my first piece of information for you. But,' he smiled, 'the Wall has been here for years, and your training is, as I've already said, the best in the world. You are the best in the world. This country is the best in the world. We have prevailed, we do prevail, we will prevail. This we know to be true. However,' his tone sad now, regretful, more-in-sorrow-than, 'there are those among us who do not see things the same way. There are those who see our desire for security, for safety, for peace' – he stretched out his arms in a gesture people often made when they were talking about the Wall, as if the Wall was like a giant pair of outspread arms – 'as a selfish desire. A selfish, self-interested turning away from the world. A refusal of our responsibilities. A – well, there's no point going on. You can't argue with people who want you to drown, to be overrun, to be washed away. You can't argue! There's nothing you can tell them to make them change their mind. And yet, they are there, and we have information that some of them, some of these deluded[1] people, are doing something almost impossible to believe. They are taking the side, not of the ordinary decent people of this country, the people you Defenders guard and protect, the people for whom you spend your long nights and days on the Wall, the people whose security is the meaning and purpose of what you do – no, they don't take their side.' He was getting into it now. He dropped his voice to a loud, histrionic[2] whisper. 'They take the side of the Others!'

1 delude sb.: deceive sb., mislead sb. **2** histrionic: dramatic, exaggerated

After dropping that, he leant back from the podium and let it sink in. 'Yes. They take the side of the Others. The Others! They would rather be on the side of the Others than on the side of their own people. It is hard to imagine such wickedness. Hard to imagine being so wrong, so morally lost, so ethically destitute[1]. I know that decent people will find it difficult to believe. But we must accept that these lost souls exist and that they are, there is no other way of putting this, on the side of the Others. And what is more, and this is the new information that we now have, they are taking steps to help the Others. There is intelligence that some of these, I would call them criminals except that most criminals are just citizens who have lost their direction in life, made some mistakes, gone awry[2] – I will instead call them what they are, traitors. These traitors are working on ways of helping the Others. Of getting the Others away from us if they succeed in getting over the Wall. Of communicating with the Others, of suggesting places and times to attack, even, and this is the most concerning development of all, of helping them get chips, of helping them to disappear into our society if they succeed in breaching the Wall. Of helping to defeat the Wall, defeat the Defenders – that's right, helping them to defeat you!'

You know what: looking around the room, I could tell that the feeling had shifted again. We weren't that bothered. The news that more Others were coming, and coming imminently[3] – that was an issue for us. That was real. We knew what that meant. The fact that Others were getting help from inside, that they might get away from the system once they were over the Wall, that wasn't really our problem. I could tell that it was a huge issue for the baby politician and I could see why, but from a Defender's point of view, if the Other gets over you're dead anyway, so the fact of the Other getting a shiny microchip and successfully hiding from the state isn't your worry. A big deal for the Others, obviously, and for the elite, but for Defenders, an Other who had got away was no longer our concern.

1 ethically destitute: having no ethical standards **2** go awry [əˈraɪ]: go wrong
3 imminent: in the very near future

He talked for a bit more but there wasn't any further new information. The take-away was, the Others were coming and they have assistance. When he finished, we packed our stuff and got in the lorry for the drive to our next shift on the Wall. About halfway there, my head started hurting and I began feeling sick: I had stopped being drunk and my hangover had kicked in. It was a long trip. When we got to our barracks, the previous watch was still on duty: we had some time to go before our shift started. I went to bed and slept for eighteen hours.

II

THE OTHERS

13

Back at the Wall, everything was the same. It always was, physically: the same sky, the same sea, the same wind, the same horizon. Same concretewaterwindsky. But the politician had been right too. Rumours were going around that there was increased activity by the Others. More boats on the horizon, more lights at night. There was also news of attacks, three in the last two weeks. (Detailed briefings on any attack were given to all Defenders. You never knew when you might learn something that would later save your life.) The attacks had been very poorly planned and inexpert[1], basically Others just coming up to the Wall in rowing boats, asking to be killed. Remember, though, on the Wall low risk is high risk. The Captain brought us all together and gave us a lecture on exactly this topic.

'So why is this bad news? Being under attack from untrained, unarmed Others who have exactly zero chance of getting through.' I held up my hand.

'Because it means they're desperate. And if the clueless ones are desperate, the clever ones will be too.'

'Point to Chewy,' said the Captain. 'Don't let the thick[2] ones make you lower your guard. They're coming.'

Hughes held up his hand. 'Sir, any evidence of that support from collaborators that we were warned about?' he asked.

'No,' said the Captain. It was impressive how he could, just by standing still with no change of expression, call something bullshit without using the word.

So, they were coming. And yet, at any given time, on any given shift, they weren't. Not yet anyway. Three attacks on ten thousand kilometres of wall wasn't all that many attacks, when you averaged

1 inexpert (adj): *laienhaft* **2** thick (infml): stupid it out[1]. The year was heading into early summer. The longer, marginally[2] warmer days and shorter, marginally warmer nights made being on duty easier for both shifts. I had also, I realised, got through the first phase of being a Defender, the one where every shift was an assault on my sense of what was physically possible, and was now at the second stage, where you get used to it, where the rhythm of a shift is familiar, where you know that the twelve hours are going to go past, and the best thing to do is just let them: don't fight the passing of time, ride on it, float on it. Better: let it go its own way. Don't look at your watch. Think about something else. If anything happens, let your adrenaline and your training take care of it. Don't live on the edge[3]. Don't be on edge[4]. Time will pass, all you have to do is let it.

I spent many hours, that shift, thinking about the conversation I'd had with Hughes while we were camping. What did I want to be when I grew up? If I wasn't going to be a member of the elite, what was I going to do instead? I might be comrades and friends with my fellow Defenders, might feel I had things in common with them, but that didn't mean I liked or had things in common with my parents. I wasn't going to go back home. Home no longer felt like home. I'd go to college and then what? Hughes wanted to spend his life among books. I didn't. I quite liked the idea of going and living with some of my new friends, Hifa and Cooper and Shoona and Mary and Hughes, going off together and finding a new way of living, more communal[5], not family-based but where we would live together and look after each other and maybe other like-minded people would join us. We'd maybe live on a farm, we'd maybe have, you know, goats. The kind of thing farm people had.

I had to admit that I knew nothing about farming. I just liked the idea of trying something else. I didn't want to spend the rest

1 average sth. out: calculate the average of sth. **2** marginally: not very much **3** live on the edge: take unnecessary risks **4** on edge: nervous **5** communal: as part of a community

of my life in a suburban hutch[1] doing work I didn't even have the emotional energy to hate. Like my parents. When you're on the Wall, you're desperate to get off the Wall. It's all you think about: getting through your turn of duty, getting off the Wall. But then you start to think, why? What do I want to get off the Wall for? What's waiting for me?

I could just – this was the terrible, unsayable thing, the thing I would have sworn an oath was impossible, just weeks before – I could just start to see why people sometimes signed up for more than one shift on the Wall. People like Sarge and the Corporal, who were on their second turn; people like the Captain, who had done three and was now on his fourth. I'm not saying that I was starting actively to think about it. I'm just saying that I could see why people did. See that they liked the combination of long dull[2] uneventful days with a strong sense of purpose looming[3] overall; the mix of aimless time, structured days and meaningful work. A bit like human life in general, you could say, the terrible regularity with which nothing happens, the genuine terror when something does. Hurry up and wait. That's the motto which governs most lives. It's the motto which governs the Wall, for sure. The only thing worse than when nothing happens is when something does.

Or maybe I'd do a bit of both, or all three: I'd do another shift on the Wall, which would be horrible, as horrible as this one, except perhaps it would be a bit less so because I would understand what I was doing and I would be doing it not because I had to, not because I had no choice, but precisely because I did have a choice, because it was up to me, because it was in my control, and I knew what I'd be gaining by doing it. I'd be gaining a route up and out, a chance to become someone else, a chance to win privileges, like the Captain – maybe I'd be offered a chance to train as an officer, then go to college, then fight my way into the elite and zoom around on planes for a bit, go to ... do whatever it is members of the elite do, conferences

1 hutch: box in which pets are kept **2** dull: boring **3** loom (v): appear in a frightening or threatening way

or talks or meetings, big discussions about the Change, then go and start a commune and live with Hifa and the others and find a new style of living, a new balance. New things to want, new ways to be. Yes, that was a good idea, that was now my new policy, my plan: I would do a little bit of everything.

That was how my mind would wander during those nights, nights which seemed to be appreciably[1] shorter with every shift that went past. After ten days, the 'night' shift was starting in full daylight and ending in full daylight. The first coffee/snack break, Mary coming down the Wall on her bicycle cart, was just as night fell; the last visit from her, with her last coffee of the shift, was just before dawn. Right from my first day I had liked Mary's visits – there was nothing original about that, everyone loved Mary. It's hard not to like the person who comes bringing chat and laughter and company and a warm drink in the middle of a long lonely watch, but even so, her personality was perfectly adapted to the job. She was the kind of person who leaves most people smiling, most of the time. Even the look of her could make you smile, her round pretty pink face and curly near-ginger[2] hair which always seemed to be trying to escape from whatever she was wearing to control and contain it – a kerchief[3] when she was in the kitchen, a hood or a beanie or a cap when she was out, depending on the warmth and the wetness. Those long stretches of time made people cranky[4], and it was easy to have sharp swings[5] in mood, passages of time when you felt sure you weren't going to get through it. Mary never had that: her job was a relatively privileged one, by comparison, and she knew it, and made it part of her job to make everyone else feel better.

The tenth night of that shift, Mary did her second set of rounds with dawn minutes away. I watched her on her usual routine, her bike stopping in each Defender's pool of light as she came along the ramparts, cup of warm drink and a few words for everyone. That night a gale was blowing. The waves and the wind were so loud that

1 appreciably: much **2** ginger: brownish-orange colour **3** kerchief [ˈkɜːtʃɪf]: piece of cloth worn on the head **4** cranky: bad-tempered **5** swing (n): change

it was hard to hear even the communicator earpiece. A roar, the sea as loud as I had ever heard it. The Captain had already been around twice that night, not saying anything much, just checking in. It was clear that he had taken the warnings from the baby politician seriously. I don't remember exactly what I was thinking, probably just counting down to the end of the shift: four more nights, meaning it was nearly over, and then two weeks away and then two weeks of days, concretewaterwindsky, and then I'd be almost halfway through my first year on the Wall. It wasn't quite time to begin celebrating that the end was in sight, but I could at least know that I knew how to get through the time, that it would go past and then it would be over and I'd be off the Wall.

Mary stopped for a longer than usual chat with Shoona. There was a faint line at the horizon, dawn imminent, though the wind hadn't yet dipped[1] as it often does at daybreak. She got back on her bike – or rather put her feet back on the pedals, she had been straddling it during her rounds, as always – and came over to me. I took a scan of the Wall and the water and prepared to give her my full attention for the next couple of minutes.

'Oof,' she said when she arrived, 'hello darling, I swear I'm getting more unfit the longer I do this, that doesn't make sense, does it, should be the other way round. Coffee and a biscuit, not in that order. Here, hold this.' She reached into her shoulder bag and was holding out a packet of biscuits. I remember thinking: chocolate and orange jam, my favourite. I took them and put my rifle down on the bench, still within arm's reach as per the rules, and unhooked my metal cup from the outside of my rucksack while she fiddled with the thermos flask. I was glad it was coffee rather than tea, because although the tea tasted better the coffee was more effective at keeping me awake. As she reached forwards to pour it I saw she had spilt it over herself, though spilt it in a strange place, along her throat and the front top of her waterproof, and I thought, that's weird, I know she can be clumsy, but how did Mary manage to pour the coffee

1 dip (v): go down, lose strength

upwards, somehow to chuck it up over herself? She made a small noise, a bit like the 'oof' when she stopped her bike, but quieter, more involuntary; she sounded surprised. She dropped the thermos and looked down at herself and then all at once several things happened, simultaneously, but also slowly:

The liquid was a strange colour. A strange texture too. Mary was backlit[1], a lamp behind her, so I couldn't see properly, and I realised, yes, it was the texture that was wrong, not the colour: the way the wetness was thick but also moving too fast for a mere spill; it can't be coffee, can she have spilt food on herself? but no it's a liquid, but no it's wrong for water, and it's not spilling it's pumping, it's not been poured over her it's coming out of her. There's only one thing it can be, it's blood.

But how can it be blood? It's not a nosebleed, she hasn't thrown blood up on herself, my that would be a very serious illness, one that had you throwing blood up on yourself, anyway it's not coming out of her mouth it's coming from further down, it's pumping out of her, it's—

I swear I can remember this whole train of thought, a line of argument running through my mind as if I was, I don't know, defending a PhD thesis[2] or something. It can only have taken a tiny fraction of a second, and then I understood: Mary had been hit by a bullet or a knife or something similar, it was a very bad wound that she probably wouldn't survive. We were under attack. The Others had come.

I went for my rifle and dived[3] behind the bench, looking at the Wall. I don't remember saying or doing anything to raise the alert, but afterwards during the debrief they played back recording of all communications that night, and the evidence is right there in the form of my voice, slightly raised but not, I'm proud to say, panicky: I sound the way you sound when you're giving an order at the window of a drive-through fast-food place, and you speak louder than usual to make sure they get the order right. 'Section twelve under

1 backlit: with light shining from behind **2** PhD thesis: *Doktorarbeit* **3** dive: (here) jump down

attack, Others, code red' – code red meaning this is not a drill, this is not a warning, they're right here, right now. On the recording you can hear, about five seconds later, the full alert alarm go off: at this point the other shift would be waking up, running to the armoury, and then running for the Wall. I remember hearing gunfire off to my left, not far away, maybe only one post over (that would be Shoona) and I remember looking – and at this I was a little frantic[1], for sure – to see where the Others were, the Others who were near enough to have killed Mary but not yet in sight. I saw a glinting metal thing on top of the Wall and in that slowed-down, point-by-point analytic process, worked out what it must be. Metal object, not there before. Must belong to the Others. Don't recognise it. Steel painted black. A claw[2] shape, like a crab: a grapple[3]. Others coming up Wall using grapple. I wonder, what should I do about that? I know, I'll run to the Wall and shoot whoever is on the other side, because if I wait until they get to the top, they will shoot me instead. I heard gunfire, frantic uncontrolled gunfire, from further down the ramparts. Somebody was shooting on full automatic, not firing short bursts the way we'd been trained, but emptying the whole magazine in one go. I stepped towards the Wall and then just at the last moment, the very last moment, remembered my training, that if I suspected Others at a specific point I should go a few metres away and look from there, because they'd be waiting to see my head pop over the parapet[4] exactly above the spot they were climbing, and would blow my head off.

I ran five metres down the Wall, knelt, and popped my head over just enough to see, for the shortest fraction of a second. The far side of the Wall was in deep shadow and I couldn't see well but there were shapes on the Wall, one of them near the top: three of them, I thought, though it could have been four if there were two together at the bottom. I had a few seconds before the first figure would get over the Wall. I ran ten metres back the other way, so I

1 frantic: hectic, in panic **2** claw: nail of an animal's foot **3** grapple (n): *Wurfhaken* **4** parapet: *Brüstung, Balustrade*

was five metres past my post, on the other side from where I'd taken the sighting: the idea being that if they'd seen me they'd expect me to pop up and start shooting from the same spot. I took a breath, stood, and emptied half the magazine into the first figure, then the other half into the Others who were below. I was sure I'd killed the first one because, although he made no sound that I could hear over the noise of my weapon, he let go his grip and fell back into the sea. I wasn't sure if I'd hit the other two or three. I ducked back down the Wall and ran back to the first point I'd used to look over. I loaded a second magazine. As I stood to shoot, I felt a blow like a heavy punch on the upper right of my back, just below the shoulder. I turned, this was in Shoona's direction, and saw three Others, one of them kneeling and aiming a weapon, the closer two running towards me.

I tried to raise my rifle to shoot them but nothing happened. I was very aware of how time had slowed down, so the first thing I thought was that this was just an extreme version of the same phenomenon, that my brain had sent the command for my arm to lift, but the arm hadn't responded yet. This thought seemed perfectly normal, as if I was in one of those video games where the protagonist can slow down time and the player has plenty of opportunity to aim, think, calibrate, during a moment which in real life would be mere hundredths of a second. My arm will be moving soon, I told myself, I've given the instruction, I've ordered it to move, so it will be raising the rifle to aiming position any moment now ... and yet nothing happened, and I realised that time had not slowed down to the extent I thought it had, because the Others were still running towards me, and the one who had been kneeling to aim a weapon had now got up and was starting to run towards me too. I'd been wounded in my right arm and couldn't raise it. I reached across to lift my rifle with my left hand, but even as I did so I was thinking, who am I kidding, these guns aren't designed to be used one-handed, I can't aim and shoot with one arm, it just isn't possible, and that means I can't defend myself and that means I'm going to die here, today, in this very minute that I'm living through right now, so this is the last night I'll ever see, these are the last sounds I'll ever hear, the last thing in front of my eyes in this lifetime is going to be this Other forty metres away who has stopped and steadied himself and is aiming a rifle at me, here we go, he's aiming, I'm going to die right—

The Other's head disappeared. No other word for it. He was standing in silhouette, aiming, then he was still standing, except his body ended at the shoulders and neck. Time slowed again and he stood still for the longest time, a grotesque statue, but while he was standing still, or the thing which used to be him was standing still, everything else was noise and movement. A huge explosion came from just below my position on the Wall, and then as I was staggering[1] and reeling[2] from it, another. Earlier in the fight I had had some understanding of what was happening, but by now I had lost it, and had no idea what was going on: if I'd been more aware, less disoriented and (to be fair to myself) not bleeding heavily from the wound in my shoulder and back, I might have realised that was Hifa, ignoring the rules about grenade launcher use and shooting the Others who were climbing the Wall by my post. In front of me, where the first Other had lost his head, I saw the Captain, running up the inside steps onto the ramparts, swinging a huge knife, not a standard bayonet but a giant thing, a machete, into the back of one of the two surviving Others. He had emptied his magazine into the head of the man who had been about to kill me and now his only weapon was this knife. The last Other turned towards him and started to raise his rifle. If he had been running with it in his hands, the Captain would have died; but that fraction of a second it took to raise-and-aim killed the Other. The Captain jumped towards him and swung his machete into the Other's neck. It was not a clean cut, the huge knife stuck in the man's throat and he staggered sideways, dropping his gun and raising his arms to his neck, apparently trying to pull the metal out of his body. I watched this with what felt like objectivity and detachment[3], thinking: if I were in his position, I too

1 stagger (v): walk unsteadily **2** reel (v): walk unsteadily **3** detachment: feeling of having no connection to what is going on around you

would attempt to remove the machete from my neck, so I understand this man's reasoning, but I am not confident he will be able to achieve his goal. He staggered back across in the other direction, away from the Captain, and then fell forwards. He did not lie still; he writhed[1] around on the ground. The Captain stepped over to the Other's rifle, picked it up, moved to stand over him, and fired a short burst into him to kill him.

It was quiet, or rather, the gunfire had stopped. I could hear voices, Defenders' voices, from down the Wall. At some point in the fight my communicator earpiece had become detached and I was cut off from the general chatter, if there was any. At some other point I had sat down and leant with my back against the Wall. I saw that I had taken my glasses off and put them down beside me. I put them back on. The attack seemed to be over. I could tell because if it had still been continuing the Captain would have run in the direction of the fighting. Instead he came over to me and bent down. He was breathing heavily but otherwise seemed calm. He reached to touch my arm then stopped.

'You're wounded,' he said. He stepped back and spoke into his communicator and it seemed mere seconds later that a military ambulance came alongside the inner ring road and two corpsmen[2] jogged up the Wall. It wasn't until this point that, like a switch[3] being toggled[4], I was abruptly in pain. It started in my right shoulder and spread all down my right side. It was an anthology[5] of pain types compressed together, at the same time dull and sharp and stabbing and throbbing[6] and gripping.

'Take good care of this one, he did well tonight,' the Captain said to the medics. I didn't know at the time, but that was to be the only compliment he ever paid me. They put me on the stretcher and car-

1 writhe [raɪð]: move your body because you are in pain **2** corpsman: member of a military medical unit **3** switch (n): button **4** toggle sth.: press sth. **5** anthology: collection **6** throb (v): pulsate

ried me down to the ambulance and hooked me up to various tubes, and the pain began to subside[1].

Time now began running at a completely different speed. During the fight each split second gave you time to think, to see what was coming, to consider alternatives and consequences in the moment between pulling a trigger and the bullet coming out of the barrel. Then there was a short passage of time when I was in the moment, during the moment, time passing at the right speed, which was roughly now, as I got into the ambulance. After that, the next few days went past in a blur of tubes and pills and tests and proddings[2] and doctors, interrupted by passages when senior members of the Border Defence Force (too important to be mere Defenders) came and gravely, respectfully asked repetitive questions about what had happened that night.

While they asked questions, they also answered mine, or some of them. That's how I found out what happened. We had been attacked by twelve Others, who went after posts 8, 10 and 12, Cooper and Shoona and me. They had used inflatables to get within a few hundred metres of the Wall and had then swum the last bit. They used suction devices[3] to attach to the Wall initially, then the same kit climbers use on rock faces. The fact that it was a noisy, windy night had been crucial: they had probably been waiting for that. They were trained and competent. They were from sub-Saharan Africa. It was quite likely that they had been professional soldiers in their previous lives. They had used crossbows[4] as their first weapon, for the silence. Then they switched to guns. The guns had been taped and sealed to keep out the water. The plan had been to get as many of us as possible before they started making noise. A good plan. It was a crossbow bolt[5] that had killed Mary and another one that had hit me. Shoona too had been wounded by a crossbow and then killed in the subsequent firefight. Cooper had been shot and was badly

1 subside: get less, go away **2** prodding (n): act of testing sb.'s reactions by prodding him (e.g. his knee) with a small instrument **3** suction device: *Ansaugvorrichtung* **4** crossbow: *Armbrust* **5** bolt (n): arrow of a crossbow

wounded and might not survive. Two other Defenders had died. All of the Others had been killed. So none of us would be put to sea.

On the third morning, when I was still out of it, the Captain came around to visit, accompanied by the baby politician who had given the talk at training camp, and by a senior non-baby politician whose name I did not catch. 'Well done,' they said, with variations. They gave me a piece of paper which apparently was a form of official commendation[1]. Not that it meant anything: the only prize worth having would have been remission from more time on the Wall, and that wasn't on offer. It was a pretty short visit and I was feeling woozy all the way through.

I woke up on the fourth morning with a clear head. Another toggled switch: pain subsided, brain fog gone. Hifa was sitting at the end of my bed, fiddling with her communicator. She was wearing a dressing gown. On the table beside her I could see that she had brought a box of chocolates, which she had opened and was now eating.

'I'm guessing those were supposed to be for me,' I said.

'Oh hi,' she said, looking up and blushing slightly. 'No, they were for me actually. I've been in here too. Small wound but they kept me in for observation. Concussion[2]. They're letting me out today.'

'You broke the rules on use of the grenade launcher.'

'I did, didn't I?'

She took another chocolate.

'It's surprisingly nice in here,' Hifa said. I hadn't noticed this, but looking around, I could see that it was true. The bed and chairs were much better made than anything we got as standard on the Wall; there was a view of distant hills. Even having a single room was a luxury. The room had a bath and toilet. There was Help. You were brought three meals a day. You had your own television. It was certainly a pleasanter place to be than the barracks. 'Almost worth it,' Hifa added.

'For concussion maybe, but some of us got shot.'

1 commendation: award **2** concussion: *Gehirnerschütterung*

'Well, by a crossbow – not sure that counts as being shot.'

'Tell Mary that,' I said, and realised as soon as the words were out of my mouth that it was the wrong thing to say, horribly wrong, not fair to Hifa and not fair to Mary, and if I thought about it for long enough, not fair to myself. Hifa's face changed and I could see her feelings churning[1], the fear and loss and grief, and by seeing them in her I could suddenly locate them in myself too. Mary was dead, had died in her own blood standing three feet away from me, and Shoona had died too, in terror and in pain, and maybe Cooper was going too, to join all the others who died that night, and me so nearly among them, death so near in those moments I could stretch out and touch the hem of its coat. I hadn't been having any feelings about what had happened – I suppose I just hadn't been ready to. Now I felt terrified, of the night itself – frightened of what I had already been through, which makes no sense, but that is what I felt – and with it had a sick sense of apprehension of going back to the Wall and living through it all again.

'Sorry,' I said, but although she had tears in her eyes, she just shook her head, apology not needed, she understood. It can happen, when you spend all your time with a group of people, that interaction between you gets stuck; there's a particular register[2] in which all your exchanges happen. With Defenders, there was stand-your-ground joshing, banter[3] which could be aggressive and could be defensive but was never not there: a wall of its own. There were hardly any times when you were just plainly and defencelessly yourself with other people. That could make certain sorts of conversation difficult to have. Hughes talking about what he wanted to do after the Wall – that was an unusual thing. Now, in this moment with Hifa, I felt a physical barrier between me and whatever was supposed to happen next. I didn't know what to say other than that I had no idea what to say. I hadn't meant to hurt her feelings. I hadn't meant to hurt my own feelings, for that matter. I didn't want to make a joke about Mary, whose death had been the worst thing

1 churn (v): move violently **2** register (n): way of speaking **3** banter (n): joking

I had ever seen, the worst thing I ever hoped to see. Hifa had been trying to banter with me, I had been trying to do the same back, and we had both messed it up. I could see that she thought, felt, the same; see too that neither of us knew what to say next. We sat for a little while, alternating looking at each other and looking at the floor, both feeling pretty miserable.

'I'm sick of the Wall,' Hifa eventually said.

'Me too.'

'If we stay on the Wall, and the attacks keep happening, and the attacks are like that, we'll eventually die.'

'Maybe.'

And then she said something which I have to admit I didn't expect:

'Do you want to Breed with me?'

14

You may know in general that the nation needs more babies, and you may know that it encourages people to Breed, but you don't know the half of it until you actually set up in business as a Breeder yourself. Breeders, or people trying to Breed, get special quarters on the Wall. They get rooms to share. In addition to the room and the extra rations you also get some say[1] in where you want to serve your time on the Wall, and the ability to change shifts. In other words you can move away from the place and the squad you were previously with – as far as I know, becoming a Breeder is the only way you get to have any say in that. A pretty sweet deal. If you could get used to the thought of bringing another person into the broken world. I can honestly say that the idea had never crossed my mind, before Hifa suggested it, and then as soon as she had, I knew I had no choice. It was the closeness of death – that was what did it. We could save ourselves from dying by bringing somebody new into the world. It suddenly seemed like the only thing to do.

There were lots of good things about Breeding, or trying to. Some of them I won't spell out[2] here. I'll just say Hifa and I turned out to be a good fit[3]. Being wanted by someone who wants you, and then getting what you want ... nothing in the world is quite like that. There was only one downside to the new turn in our relationship, which was that the other members of our squad thought it was hilarious, and wouldn't stop teasing us about it. People were in a bad place[4], after the attack and the deaths, and me and Hifa hooking up[5] was the only other thing to talk and think about apart from how dis-

1 get some say in sth. (infml): *ein Mitspracherecht bei etw. bekommen* **2** spell sth. out: explain sth. in detail **3** fit (n): match **4** be in a bad place (infml): be in a bad mood, have a difficult time **5** hook up with sb. (infml): start having a relationship with sb.

traught everyone was, so that's all that they did: tease us and make jokes at us and ask us if the baby was on the way yet and if we were having fun trying and if we had tried doing it this way, that way, would we like someone else to try in my place, would we like the whole squad to watch to make helpful comments on technique and form, had we given any thought to what we would do if the baby was Chinese, etc., etc., et bloody cetera.

During the next few weeks, it was as if I had two lives. One of them, the best and realest, was with Hifa. The two of us were excused training – my injury, plus our new aspiring Breeder privileges – and we spent a whole week entirely together. We knew each other very well, had spent more time in each other's company than a lot of couples who are just starting out; we had shared the most intense experience of our lives together. But from another perspective, we hardly knew each other at all. We had never had an argument. We had never seen each other naked. I didn't know anything about her family other than that she was no keener on seeing them than I was on seeing mine. So we started to find out those things, to do those things, to get to know each other differently/deeper/better. I liked that, in fact I loved it.

In parallel: the Wall. That life which had felt like the realest thing I would ever do now seemed like a backdrop[1] for my other, realer, private life. Many things changed. For a start, we were moved off it for a four-week section of training and reserve duty. With four dead and three injured from one squad of fifteen, we needed to be restaffed[2] and retrained: to settle in the new people and wait for me and Hifa to be ready for active duty. In the middle of that period I was, of all things, given a medal. It turned out that the certificate from the baby politician was a promissory note[3] telling me that there was more to come.

The whole company went in a lorry to a town about half an hour's drive away from our temporary barracks. We stopped around

1 backdrop: background **2** restaff: get new staff to replace those that are gone
3 promissory note: *Schuldschein*

the back of the town hall and were met by some Help who led us through a winding[1] series of corridors to suddenly come out on stage in front of a few hundred seated civilians. There was bunting[2] above the podium; there was a television camera pointed at us. The loudspeaker system played pop music from the recent past while we waited. Then there was a bustle[3], a movement among the functionaries running the event, and a person who was obviously important came through the door we had come through and went up to the podium. People cheered and clapped. I had no idea who he was, but the civilians obviously did. He must have been a member of the elite who was clever at being popular with ordinary people. He held up his hands and people went quiet and then he made a mesmerising[4] speech about the Wall (he called it the National Coastal Defence Structure) and the Defenders and how important we are and what heroes we are and how Britain is a nation of heroes and how our heroism is in the finest tradition of British heroism and how heroic that is. I may be misremembering some of this: we all agreed it was a great speech though afterwards we found it hard to repeat anything he'd said. Basically, there was lots in it about heroism and how we were heroes. Our names were read out, and we went up in order and were given the medals. The politician pinned them onto our uniforms. I was third out of five up to the podium. The Captain got a more important medal, and Hifa and one other squad member who had killed Others got smaller medals. I'd never stood in front of a roomful of people applauding me before, and don't ever expect to do it again. It's embarrassing to admit (though why is it embarrassing?) but I really liked it.

Then the ceremony was over and we were invited to a reception room[5] upstairs and a selection of the audience came up too and there was Help serving everyone with drinks and small snacks, and being Defenders, we tried to get as many of the drinks down

1 winding (adj): with several curves **2** bunting: little flags for decoration
3 bustle (n): nervous movement **4** mesmerising (adj): fascinating, captivating
5 reception room: *Empfangszimmer*

us as we could. There was one glass of wine each, only the second time I've ever had wine because it became rare and expensive after the Change, but there was plenty of beer and gin and whisky and most of us managed to get properly hammered in the thirty minutes we were there, the kind of abrupt, vertical-take-off drunkenness where you get so much alcohol on board so quickly you grow steadily drunker for the next couple of hours. A great night out. Hifa started feeling ill on the lorry home and when we got to barracks she went into our loo[1] and I held her hair back while she was sick and I realised that I loved her and that I'd never felt so happy. I think that was the best day of my life.

1 loo (BE, infml): toilet

15

'We're going to Scotland,' said the Captain. There was a rumbling[1] and shifting in the briefing room. The entire company was there, in its new form, a mix of old Defenders and replacements. He let the news marinate[2] for a few moments.

'You may be wondering why,' he went on. Speaking for myself, I wasn't, not particularly; if you look for logic on the Wall you're not far away from expecting the process to be fair, and if you expect it to be fair, you start to go mad. That's my take on it anyway. So, no wondering why for me. 'The reason is, this squad is considered to have done its fair share of the hard work of defending our frontiers. Here in the south is the first line of attack and the first line of defence.' He meant, the first line of defence from the Others, but didn't say so. I had noticed before that he used the word 'Others' as little as possible. It was the only sign he gave of sensitivity about his former life, his former self. 'In the north, it is different. The reasons for this are simple. The people attempting to cross the Wall are coming from a southerly direction. The journey to the north is therefore longer and more dangerous. The north is also colder. That means that there are fewer attempts to penetrate our defences from that direction. That means that defending the Wall is, in practice, less difficult in the far north. Sergeant, what maxim[3] am I about to quote?'

Sarge had been cut on his face on the night of the attack, and the wound had not fully healed. It was spectacular, a double line of stitches down his right cheekbone, on either side of a livid[4] scar. Half a centimetre higher and he would have lost his eye. As it was

1 rumbling (n): low sound **2** let sth. marinate (infml): let sth. sink in **3** maxim: well-known phrase **4** livid: with a dark colour

the scar made his expression look permanently contorted[1] with disbelief: he looked like a stocky[2], angry, sceptical pirate.

'Less risky is more risky,' he said.

'Yes. So bear that in mind. The idea that the north is harder to attack, easier to defend, may in itself be a factor which draws attacks. Still,' he said, easing off the intensity a little, 'we are being sent there for some respite[3], and it's to be hoped that we'll find it. As summer arrives the days are very long and the nights very short. We have a chance to get to know each other as a new company. We may well, after a period in the far north and further training, be transferred back to the south. My advice would be to make the most of it. We train, then we go north at the next deployment.'

'He seemed almost cheerful,' Hifa said later. We were putting away our kit to go on a week's leave. The company had been on standby duty near our barracks. I wasn't fit enough to fight but I was on administrative duties while I recovered: which meant, doing chores for the Captain, Sergeant and Corporal. It was uninteresting but not difficult. 'I wonder what the secret bad news is.'

'Cold?' I said. 'Remote?' Hifa shrugged. She held out her hand to me and I took it. We were setting out to do something we had long discussed and Hifa had long dreaded.

'Are you sure you're ready for this?' she said.

'I think so.'

'You can say if you aren't.'

'I know.'

'I won't hold it against you and bring it up later.'

'I know.'

'I have doubts of my own.'

'I understand.'

'It's not guaranteed to go well.'

'Yes, I understand.'

1 contorted (adj): twisted **2** stocky: having a short but strong body **3** respite (n): short break

'Not through any fault of yours – please don't think that. It's just, it could go wrong.'

'I know.'

'I don't want to have misled you.'

'Thank you.'

'To make it clear.'

'OK, Hifa, I've got it, I really have, and if you think it's a bad idea and don't want me to do it that's completely fine, we won't.'

'No need to be arsey[1].'

'I don't think I was.'

'Well that's a matter of opinion.'

'Hifa, for fuck's sake, we're only talking about visiting your mother for a few days. She isn't Hitler. At least if she was Hitler I assume you'd have said.'

She exhaled, slow and long.

'I just, I don't want it to get in the way,' she said, more subdued[2], less fighty[3].

'It won't,' I said. 'I promise.'

We took the usual journey at the end of that shift, lorry to train to London. We were leaving Ilfracombe 4 for ever. The company was the quietest and the soberest I'd ever seen it on a trip like this. The new people hadn't really bedded in[4] yet and the Defenders who'd been there for longer were all thinking about the people who weren't with us. Absent friends. There was still no news about Cooper. It was odd, because if you had pumped me full of truth serum and asked me if there was anything about that section of the Wall I would miss – the section where we'd spent the winter months in the cold and dark, where I'd been the most frightened I'd ever been, and the most bored I'd ever been, and had the most intense experiences of my life, and nearly died – I'd have said no. But as we left it behind and it moved into the past, moved into the category of experiences which were over, I realised I felt a sense of loss. I'd probably never

1 arsey (infml): unfriendly **2** subdued: in a quiet and controlled way **3** fighty (infml): aggressive **4** bed in (infml): become part of the team

see it again: that particular stretch of concretewindwatersky, that exact patch of damp over my bed, those precise stretches of ramparts where puddles would accumulate in the gravel. The place where I met Hifa.

At London we split up as usual, said muted goodbyes. Hifa and I crossed the city to catch a train to the eastern town where her mother lived. The transport dynamic was always the same: on the train from the coast, where we outnumbered the civilians, we were the dominant force, the top dogs, and people were wary[1], kept away and moved away. In the city, in small numbers and as individuals, we were objects of curiosity instead of fear: people snuck glances[2] at us, observed us, would sometimes catch our eye. Nothing made you feel the gap between us and civilians more than being in the middle of them. They just weren't thinking about the same things, didn't have the same priorities, had no idea how lucky they were.

You could tell pretty much without exception when the people checking you out had been Defenders: they were a certain age, within a decade or two of us, and they looked both more empathetic and more assessing. They were probably wondering how long we'd been on the Wall, how long we had to go. I still had my arm in a sling[3] and I was wearing my medal and I could see them noticing both of those things. The look in their eyes had some pride in it, pride for you and a little bit for themselves, too; some sympathy[4] (it was easy to see them thinking, thank God I don't have to do that again, I wonder how long the poor sods have to go). Sometimes I thought I caught them thinking: when I was on the Wall, I used to tell myself I'd never forget how horrible it is to be cold and tired and frightened and have months more of the feeling to go, and I promise I'll remember this moment, and if I ever get off the Wall and remember this moment I promise I'll never again take for granted being comfortable and safe and somewhere other than here. I didn't blame them for it, I'd had

1 wary: cautious **2** sneak a glance at sb.: secretly take a quick look at sb.
3 sling: cloth that is used to support an injured arm **4** sympathy: compassion, feeling of being sorry for sb.

the same thought many times myself. I hoped more than anything to get to a point in my life when I was like them – when I had the luxury and privilege of having been away from the Wall for so long that I needed external prompts to be reminded of it. When the Wall would be in the past, not the present and the future.

The train to the east was old and slow. I liked it, the creakiness[1] and old-fashionedness of it; the kind of train where people were going home with shopping bags, but had brought their own packed snacks for the trip rather than buying anything expensive in the big city. Hifa and I didn't talk much. I watched London go past out the window and then blur into suburb and exurb[2], those random tower blocks which spread on the outskirts of the city, and then fields and country. I'm a city boy and the country always seems so empty, so underpopulated; even now when we grow all our own food and there's more said about farming and food than ever before, you never actually see any people working on the land. Drones and bots, yes, people, no.

We arrived at the end of the main line and went to the station cafe to wait for the train to the coast. We drank heavily stewed tea and ate dry biscuits which were borderline inedible[3] until you dunked them. I felt sad, suddenly and unexpectedly, and couldn't tell why, then realised I was having a near-memory of Mary, bringing her hot drinks to us twice a shift. I didn't want to say that to Hifa so I just sat there with the feelings for a moment, then looked over at her and could see she was doing something similar, sitting there staring down into her tea.

The train to the coast was even racketier[4] and smaller and older than the last one, no more than two carriages long. The fields were big and dominated by huge single crops, most of which I didn't recognise, apart from the loud yellow of rapeseed[5]. The light began to

1 creakiness: condition that causes sth. to make creaking noises all the time
2 exurb (n): area in the environs of a city that is further away from the city and less densely populated than the city's suburbs **3** borderline inedible (infml): almost not eatable **4** rackety: in a bad state **5** rapeseed: *Raps*

change as we got nearer the coast, and before long I could smell the sea. The train made frequent stops and was almost empty when it began to slow down and Hifa said, 'We're here.' She swung her ruck-sack down off the space above her seat. Hifa was not looking at all like herself, as if she had shrunk slightly. I recognised the symptoms of familial dread.

At the end of the platform, a woman with a turban wrapped complicatedly around her head and two different brightly coloured shawls was standing waiting for us, leaning on a stick. She had the same caramelly skin tone as Hifa but was taller and more operatic[1], both in how she dressed and how she acted: she projected drama. To the side of her and one pace behind was standing a woman instantly recognisable as Help.

'Darling!' she said as soon as she saw us. 'Darling! Let me look at you.' Hifa stood and submitted to this. Her mother reached out and touched her face and turned it slightly from side to side. She held her fingers over the place on the top of her head where Hifa had had stitches. She took a step backwards and looked at Hifa up and down. She tilted her own head.

'As beautiful as ever,' she said. She came over and stood in front of me. She held the cane[2] out behind her and the Help took it. Then she held out both of her hands in front of her. I felt I had no choice except to do the same. She took my hands and held them. We still hadn't spoken. She did the same up-and-down thing she had done with her daughter, then let go of my hands, and without touching me held her fingers over the place where I'd been wounded. Then she stepped back and turned to Hifa.

'Yes,' she said. 'I understand.' And to both of us: 'Welcome!'

Hifa's mother lived in a cottage ten minutes' walk from the train station. The little house stood in a row of similar properties just outside the coastal village. It was small and pretty on the outside, painted white, with a wooden gate, a trellis[3] of flowers on the front

1 operatic: like in an opera **2** cane (n): stick **3** trellis: construction used to support growing plants

wall and a small garden. The house would once have had a view of the sea, but that was now blocked by the Wall. The inside was decorated with African art and bright paintings by Hifa's mother: she had been an art teacher but retired early and was now an artist. Her speciality was painting the spirit animals of her family and friends, and she said that she was looking forward to painting mine, once she had worked out what it was.

Hifa's mother's big news was about her domestic arrangements. 'I know it's terrible to have Help,' she said, once we had got to the cottage and she had sent the Help to the shops in search of missing dinner ingredients. 'If you had said when I was younger that I would have Help, not that it existed in those days, but had explained to me what it is and that I would one day be making use of it, I would not have believed you. Another human being at one's beck and call[1], just by lifting a finger, simply provided to one, in effect one's personal property ... though of course they are technically the property of the state, there are all sorts of monitorings[2] and safeguards[3], it isn't at all like such arrangements in the benighted[4] past, it is a form of providing welfare and shelter and refuge to the wretched of the world – but no, still, I would not have believed you. It is a falling away, a lessening of one's own humanity. A decline in one's own standards. But what could I do? I had you coming, I am not getting any younger, please don't say anything polite' – this was addressed to me, though the truth is I hadn't been going to say anything in the first place – 'we both know it's true. The spirit is willing but the flesh is weak, and if we're being completely honest the spirit isn't always willing either. Age is a terrible thing, a terrible opponent. People of your time in life don't understand this but you come to find it to be true, perhaps the only thing which is true for all humans everywhere, the terribleness of age. Our deepest piece of common humanity.'

1 at sb.'s beck and call: always ready to obey sb.'s orders **2** monitoring (n): check **3** safeguard (n): protection, safety mechanism **4** benighted: backward, uncultured

I suddenly got it. Hifa's mother was one of those people who like life to be all about them. With the Change, that is a harder belief to sustain[1]; it takes much more effort to think that life is about you when the whole of human life has turned upside down, when everything has been irrevocably changed for everyone. You can do it, of course you can, because people can do anything with their minds and their sense of themselves, but it takes work and only certain kinds of unusually self-centred people can do it. They want to be the focus of all the drama and pity and all the stories. I could tell that she didn't like it that younger people are universally agreed to have had a worse deal than her generation. I understood Hifa's dread and found myself reaching for her hand. Hifa took mine, limply[2], reluctantly. I was about to find out why.

'Ah – love. The love of a partner. The sweetest thing in life, to have it, to be possessed of it. The greatest of sadnesses to look back on, in later life, in adversity, the cruel twist that your greatest happinesses become your greatest pain.' Then she leant forwards – the cottage rooms were small, so our sofa and her chair were close to each other, catty-corner[3] – and took my and Hifa's clasped hands in hers. 'Enjoy it!' she said. She got up and left the room to get her communicator to ask the Help where she was and why she was being so slow.

'Holy fuck,' I whispered to Hifa.

'You get it now.'

'Absolutely. Want me to do something? I can call Hughes, get him to call back, fake an emergency. Sudden summons[4] back to the Wall. We can, I don't know, go and stay in a B & B.'

'Or we could just kill ourselves, that would work too,' said Hifa. Then she squeezed my hand and let go. 'This too shall pass. She'll ease off from now, it's worse when she's nervous.'

That proved true. The Help came back from the shops and served an absolutely delicious cream tea, an old-school treat that I'd heard

1 sustain sth.: uphold sth., maintain sth. **2** limply: with little energy **3** catty-corner (infml): diagonally opposite each other **4** summons (n): order to return

of but never had, with fresh scones[1] (Hifa's mother: 'made under my direction') and fresh clotted cream[2], and jam made by Hifa's mother the previous autumn. I made the mistake of asking for the recipe, out of nothing but politeness, which gave her the opportunity to say: 'The balance of sugar and sharpness has to be just right, as sweet as love, as bitter as loss.' There would be these moments when Hifa's mother suddenly went off on one. The rest of the time she was OK, and she could be very funny, especially about her neighbours. Also, as always, it was good to be away from the Wall and especially so to be with Hifa. We went for a walk down to what had been the sea-front and was now a strange marooned[3] parade of shops in the lee[4] of the Wall, their facades oriented towards a promenade and a view which were no longer there. We did a lot of walking that weekend, as a device for getting out of the house.

'How come she can afford Help?'

'I haven't asked but I can guess. Dad sends her money. He felt guilty about going off and leaving her – leaving us. He had to pay child support, but even when he didn't have to any more, he still sent cheques.'

'She told you that?'

Hifa gave me a look.

'Of course not. He did.'

'I thought you never saw him?'

'I don't. Hardly. Anyway, she's canny[5] with money, always has been. When she was working she saved.'

'I feel a bit sorry for the Help. More sorry than usual, I mean.'

'Yeah – I wouldn't be at all surprised if she decided to swim for it.'

I laughed. Being with Hifa's mother made me think about my parents; about the difference between me and them, so different from Hifa and her mother, and yet maybe not, at the same time.

1 scone: type of bread roll **2** clotted cream: very thick and fatty cream usu. eaten with scones **3** marooned (adj): deserted **4** lee: *Windschatten* **5** canny: clever

Who broke the world? They wouldn't say that they did. And yet it broke on their watch[1].

Hifa was right, though: it did get easier. Her mother dialled it down[2] a bit. That gave Hifa the chance to relax a little and as she did she told me about her childhood, the dad who was great when he was there but was prone[3] to go away without warning, until one day he never came back; the charismatic, flaky[4], loving, difficult mother. The small-life country childhood which makes you need to get away so badly you can feel it in the roots of your hair. We wandered all over the town and the countryside around it. The paradox was that you couldn't see the sea when you were close to it, because of the Wall, but if you went for a walk inland, and climbed up a bit, you could. So you went inland to see the sea. I was at that point of recovery when you feel annoyed by your own weakness; when you are bored, as a prelude to getting better. Bored with my physical condition, I mean. In other respects I was feeling better than ever. I was imagining a future off the Wall, once we were pregnant. We'd find work, take turns looking after the baby, maybe take turns going to college, and it would be onwards and upwards. There would be a new life, and we would be living a new life. It felt like too much to hope for, but not in a bad way, more the kind of thing you stop yourself thinking about for superstitious reasons, because if you let yourself imagine all the details, it's less likely to happen. Breeders got good accommodation, so I wouldn't have to go back to live with my parents and Hifa wouldn't have to go back to live with hers.

By the fourth day of that week, my arm was out of its sling, and my shoulder, though it still hurt, hurt in a specific numb way which was unlike the access-all-areas pain I'd had when I was wounded. Unexpectedly catching a glimpse of myself in the mirror – there were lots of mirrors in the cottage – I thought, who's that good-looking dude, then realised it was me, looking rested and well.

1 on sb.'s watch: during the time when sb. is responsible **2** dial sth. down: reduce the amount or the intensity of sth. **3** be prone to sth.: *zu etw. neigen* **4** flaky (infml): strange

At the end of the week, Hifa's mother walked us to the train station. By now we were on nodding terms[1] with the neighbours, who waved or nodded back as we walked past. She stood on the single platform and waited until the two-carriage train came in. She held our hands together and looked at us for a long time.

'Courage,' she said, tears in her eyes. 'Courage, my brave, brave darlings. I feel for you. Courage!' She squeezed hard and then let go.

'I cannot watch you go away. I will leave you now,' she said. And she marched out of the station with her cane, a handkerchief in her right hand, dabbing it to her face as she disappeared back into the town. Hifa and I got into the train.

'Well, she found a way of making it about her,' I said, and then saw that Hifa was affected too, looking sad; I'd misread the moment. We found seats, sat heavily down, and off we were yet again on that train-train-lorry journey. We pulled away from the sea and set off towards the other sea, where we'd be standing watch.

She didn't get around to painting me, but she did manage to work out my spirit animal. Apparently I'm a goat. 'A very resourceful animal – they can live on scraps[2].' She said she'd paint it next time. There never was a next time, but of course I didn't know that then.

1 be on nodding terms with sb.: know sb. well enough to nod to him/her when you see him/her **2** scrap (n): little amount of sth.

16

Defenders have a saying, 'The Wall has no accent.' It means when you're standing looking at the water, standing watching for Others, it doesn't matter where you are, it's all concretewaterwindsky:

concrete

water

wind

sky:

it's basically always the same.

Like most sayings about most things, this is partly true, partly not. Yes, the Wall is the Wall and the Others are the Others and a twelve-hour shift is a twelve-hour shift. You don't have any interaction with the locals, wherever you are. The days tick down at the same rate. But the light and wind and water are subtly different, and you get to know them so well that while you could say that the Wall has no accent you could equally say the opposite: along the ten thousand kilometres of Wall, no two posts are identical.

That was especially true in the far north. It just felt different. Longer days, slanting[1] light, different scents on the wind. It was the best time of the year to be up north, no question, and I didn't love the thought of what it would be like in winter, but then if we'd been briefed[2] correctly, we might not be there in winter, we'd be posted back down to the busy areas, once we were fully trained and ready. My view was: whatever. Hifa would be pregnant soon, and we'd

1 slanting: *schräg* **2** brief sb.: inform sb., instruct sb.

be out of there. We'd be living the Breeder life in our special state-donated[1] Breeder accommodation.

I was glad of the change for all sorts of reasons. Hughes had been switched to our shift, to give us another experienced Defender in place of the people we'd lost; that was good. He was the person I liked talking to best, after Hifa, and the quality of chat on the communicator increased exponentially. But I missed Shoona. I missed Cooper, who was still very sick and might recover, might not. I especially missed Mary. The new cook, Alan, was good at his job, in the sense that his food tasted good and there was plenty of it, but he was taciturn[2] and made no secret of the fact that he liked cycling along the ramparts in the middle of the night to bring us hot drinks no more than we liked standing on the Wall. Our squad had several new members, so the group dynamics were very different and I was, I found, now one of the elders, wounded and decorated, a veteran of action, a potential Breeder, a senior figure. That was weird. I was the one dispensing advice to the new arrivals about how to get through a shift, I was the one giving warnings about type 2 cold, I was the one telling people to watch out for the Captain's small-hours inspections, and take special care how you tape your ammo cartridges together. One morning I caught Hifa in the mirror smiling at me as I was brushing my teeth before shift. 'What?' I said.

'You're taller,' she said.

'Piss off,' I said, but what she said was true: I felt taller. I could tell that I held myself differently. I wasn't the same person I'd been when I arrived at the Wall.

A few days into that first tour up north, who should come for a visit but our old friend the blond baby politician, dispenser of intelligence briefings, platitudes and medals. He arrived on an afternoon of clammy[3], close-clinging mist, a very unpleasant day to be on the Wall. It was lucky that the north was quieter, because this was good weather for Others. Our shift gathered in the briefing

1 state-donated: provided by the state for free **2** taciturn [ˈtæsɪtɜːn]: quiet, not talking much **3** clammy: damp

room, which was the same as every other briefing room, except the maps were different. I found, sitting in front of him as he stood at the podium, that my instinctive dislike had subsided a little. That might be because he had been involved in giving me a medal, which was pretty pathetic, really; but there we were. Also, maybe, I was getting a glimpse of how a person made it into the elite, and starting to see that it was possible – not easy, but possible. A very good record on the Wall, followed by a record of proven success at college, a Breeder, a young person on an upward trajectory[1]; that was the kind of man for whom elites would budge up[2] and make room. The kind of outsider/insider they needed. I was taking more of an interest in him and seeing him more as an object of study than of simple loathing[3].

'Hello and welcome,' he started, as if he were our gracious host, the man in charge of the far north. 'We know each other of old, some of us, and some of us are new colleagues. Welcome. Well done! You are all members of the best defence force in the world, the best trained and the best staffed and the best prepared!'

I realised it was his standard speech and tuned out[4]. He would have to give it twice, since this was a normal tour on the Wall, not a training camp; once for us, once for the other shift. What must it be like, to go around the country talking to Defenders and the public, to not be part of their lives but talking to them about their lives, to be up there in the plane? A metaphorical plane in the case of this man, but still. To give orders while you were pretending just to be chatting, to boss people about by asking them if they would kindly do something for you ... Help, of course, there would be lots and lots of Help, cooking Help and cleaning Help and Help to look after the children if you had them, and driving Help and gardening Help for your big house with its self-sufficient food supply (just in case),

1 trajectory: path, direction **2** budge up: move closer together to make room for sb. **3** loathing: hatred **4** tune out: stop listening

repair and maintenance Help and odd-job[1] Help, electrical Help and painting and decorating Help ...

Now the speech had turned and he was repeating the warnings he had given at training – which, to be fair, had turned out to be true – about how there were more Others coming and they were more desperate. He also repeated the warnings about how the Others were suspected to have secret networks of support, secret sympathisers, hidden in the general population. They were thought to have new ways of getting away from the coast, maybe even new ways of getting chipped[2]. He went on for a bit more and then stopped his general briefing and invited me and the Captain and Hifa up on stage and talked for a bit about how we had been decorated in action and how lucky this squad was to have three such resolute, able Defenders, and how we were the best defence force in the world, the best trained and the best staffed and the best prepared.

We got down off the stage, and the baby politician stopped me for a word.

'Joseph,' he said to me in greeting – which was odd in itself, since nobody on the Wall called me by my given name, it was either Kavanagh or Chewy. Even Hifa called me Chewy (as well as some other things). 'Please – call me James.'

'Er, hi James.'

'How are you?' he said with the intensity dialled up. 'How *are* you?' He had put on a concerned face.

'I'm fine, thanks.'

'Wound better?'

'Yes, thanks.'

'Change of landscape welcome?'

'So, there's a thing Defenders say, the Wall has no accent. Meaning, it's sort of the same everywhere.'

'Do they? Do they say that? That's good, that's really good. No accent – yes.' He nodded two or three times. 'Well, it's good to catch

1 odd job: small job **2** get chipped: get a chip implanted up with old friends. Good to stay in touch. Let me just give you this, just in case.'

He took a card out of his top jacket pocket and handed it to me: a name and an email address. He reached out to give my arm a parting squeeze, then I saw him remembering that I had been wounded, and he wasn't clear for a fraction of a second what to do, then he either remembered it had been my right shoulder and he was aiming for my left arm, or he remembered that he had just asked me if I had recovered, so if my arm was too sore[1] to squeeze it was in a sense my responsibility not his, and went on with the gesture. I took the card, put it in my pocket, said goodbye. It was a small thing but I took it as a sign, meaning that he saw in me some of the same stuff I saw, or wanted to see, in myself. He could smell the ambition, the get-me-out-of-here scent, all over me.

I was pleased. I also felt that I needed to have a shower. Sarge took a moment to talk to me as we were going through to lunch. The rest of the squad had already gone ahead and sat down and were getting stuck in.

'You know what that plonker[2] said. We're lucky to have you?' I got my modest face ready and said that I did.

'Reckon if we really were lucky, we'd not have been attacked.' Fair enough.

Two tours went past without anything much happening. It was just past the top of high summer; short nights, with amazing northern sky colours I'd never seen before, shades of blue and purple shading into deep-blue-grey-purple and purple-off-black and deep black. Once or twice, during nights when we weren't on shift, Hifa and I even went for a walk inland to get away from the light pollution of the Wall, so we could see the stars. There were so many lights in the sky that night seemed not so much a thing of darkness as an experi-

1 sore: not fully healed **2** plonker (infml): idiot

ment in a different form of illumination, an invitation to navigate by star.

'It's beautiful up here,' Hifa said.

'In the summer.'

'It smells different.'

That was true – it did smell different. The sea smelt different. It must be that the sea flora were different, the kelp[1] and seaweed species were more pungent[2], vegetal and cabbagey[3], but not unpleasantly so. Greener, basically, it smelt greener. Of living things. It was hard not to imagine what life would be like after the Wall, when you could go on a walk whenever you felt like it and goof off whenever you felt like it and also work hard at clawing your way up in life and becoming a member of the elite and taking over the world. Also, a baby or babies plural. I liked those walks and that sky.

On our third far-northern tour, I didn't see the sky much, because I was on nights and the lights spoiled the view. It was the least difficult night guarding I've ever done, because the dark was so short and the nightfall and sunrise so long and so spectacular, a protracted[4] set-piece[5] natural show. The danger and difficulty of the tour down south seemed a long distance off. The only person who didn't appear to like being where we were was the Captain, who was the closest he ever got to being edgy[6]; as if the sense of quietness and peace and distance bothered him. He made his rounds more regularly than ever and had less than ever to say.

'Maybe it's a post-traumatic thing,' Hughes speculated one morning in the mess after a night when the Captain had come round no fewer than five times. 'He killed two people with a sodding machete. Practically cut them in half. People who maybe were not so unlike he once was. It's going to take a bit of processing.'

'He's not the type,' I said.

1 kelp: *Seetang* **2** pungent: having a strong taste or smell **3** cabbage (adj): like cabbage **4** protracted: lasting longer than usual **5** set-piece (adj): standard **6** edgy: tense, irritable

'Everyone's the type sooner or later,' said Hifa. We gently bickered[1] for a while, without reaching a conclusion. The Captain was off, though, everyone agreed.

Eight days into that tour came the first really difficult weather we had seen up north. There had been days which were damp and still, and the air was so full of moisture it was like living inside a cloud that had sunk to earth, but from the Defenders' point of view, the great virtue of that weather was that in the super-humid[2] silence, you could hear a cough or a metal clank[3] from hundreds of metres away. You could talk to the Defender at the next post without raising your voice. There were other days with abrupt squally[4] showers, gusts of wind and horizontal rain that you could see coming across the water towards you, which hit hard and overwhelmingly, and were gone in minutes. After the first one of these, you never forgot your waterproofs again. But that night was different, a hard rain and wind combined with a hard close fog; a sudden premonition of what it would be like up here when winter came.

'It's beautiful up here,' I said over the communicator.

'Oh shut up,' said Hifa.

'Get a room,' said Hughes.

'Keep it hygienic,' said Sarge, meaning, keep off the communicator unless it's to do with business. It was a sensible thing to say on a night when it was so hard to hear, but we had got a little casual up north. I don't think any of us really believed in the possibility of an attack. Sarge added: 'He hasn't been around yet, which means he'll be here any minute.' In other words, the Captain, uncharacteristically absent from his prowling so far that night, was coming soon.

I had long since given up checking the time when I was on guard, but it was some way in between 'lunch' (the midnight version of the main meal, that is) and the second cup of tea. Dawn was about an hour or more away. The weather was filthier than ever. It was hard to see. Specifically, it was hard to see straight in front of you, in the

1 bicker (v): argue **2** super-humid: very damp **3** clank (n): loud noise produced by metal hitting on metal **4** squally: *böig*

direction from which the wind and waves were coming, straight at the Wall. When you looked sideways towards the guard posts next to you, all you could see was flooding, streaming, torrential[1] rain sheeting through the Wall lights.

I remember that I was thinking, it's hard to know what's going on out there, it's like a white-out[2], except it's pitch black, when the lights failed. It was a sensation so strange, and the disorientation was so total, that it took a few seconds to understand. There was lots of swearing and lamentation over the communicator.

'This is silver command,' said Sarge, meaning, everyone else shut up. 'Hold your posts. The lights have failed all along our sector. Stand still and shut up. The backup[3] will kick in any second.'

In drills and training, the backup generator usually started within fifteen to thirty seconds. That didn't happen. It was eerie, but I wasn't worried, it was just one of those Wall cockups[4]. The thirty seconds went past, no generator, no lights, no communication. Another thirty seconds. This was the longest period of dark I'd known on the Wall since the night in training when we had been playing at attack and had used a five-minute blackout to overrun the Defenders.

The Wall lit up with gunfire. It was at the far end from my post, close to the watchtower. Several different sets of automatic weapons were firing and none of them sounded like the kind used by Defenders. Then there were three explosions, a big one, then a bigger one, then the biggest explosion I had ever seen or heard, so loud it had a shockwave that hit a second or so after the light and flame. It came from the barracks. The brief glimpse of illumination showed me nothing that I could understand, but it was clear that there was fighting on the Wall. A voice came on the communicator, saying, 'Others, code red,' which told me nothing that I didn't already know. Our training was to check if our own post was clear and then either

1 torrential: in large amounts **2** white-out (n): weather condition in which you cannot see because there is so much snow **3** backup: emergency power supply **4** cockup (infml): *Schlamassel*

obey orders or, if there weren't any, to assess whether to run towards the fight or stand at post. I stood up to the Wall but in the rain and wind and dark I couldn't see what was on the other side. There could have been an Other five feet below me, there could have been none in the next thousand metres. 'Sergeant, orders please,' I said, joining the three or four Defenders who'd made the same request, but there was no answer, so I said, 'Kavanagh post thirteen engaging[1],' and left my post to run towards the fight. There were two kinds of shooting now, our rifles and the flatter sound of the Others' weapons. Hifa said over the communicator that she was engaging too. I stopped to wait for her and thirty seconds later she was beside me, the grenade launcher at her shoulder, her eyes wild, the biggest I'd ever seen them. We just looked at each other. Then we moved off, more slowly, jogging rather than running, towards the gunfire, keeping as far away from each other as we could on opposite sides of the ramparts, to make a more difficult target.

People's eyes adapt to the dark at different speeds. Mine are pretty good. I think it took five minutes to get close to the fight and by then I could make out a group of Defenders with their backs to me, using the concrete benches as cover, and a group of Others beyond them, doing the same thing but also making darts[2] across the Wall to cross the ramparts and get down on the inner side. When people say their blood ran cold, what they're describing is the feeling of being flooded with adrenaline; it's a sensation which hits all over the body, chest to guts to limbs to heart to head. In that moment I was soaked with cold. Others had got over the Wall and were getting away. The worst thing imaginable was happening on our watch. Some of us were going to be put to sea.

When bullets come close, the noise they make as they go past changes from a zing to a crack. The bullets were starting to crack when Hifa and I got to the point where our people were fighting. Some of them were on the right of the Wall, behind a bench, and

1 engage: (here) start to fight **2** dart (n): sudden quick movement some were on the other side behind a concrete bulwark[1]. Sarge and Yos were behind the bench. We took cover with them. Three of the new people in our squad were dead on the ramparts in front of us. Four other members of the shift were in cover behind the bulwark, taking turns to fire shots. The Others were about a hundred metres from us, in the direction of the barracks. There were two vehicles on the inner side of the Wall, people carriers. I assumed they were Defenders from nearby posts come to help us, but as Hifa and I arrived one of the cars drove away, fast. I realised that the Others had assistance; the rumours of support were true. Hence the black-out. Hence maybe the explosion in our barracks.

'Where's the rest of the company?' I said to Sarge. He reached around the bench, fired off a few rounds, then turned to me.

'The barracks were sabotaged. They're dead or wounded. No help from there.'

'How many have got away?'

'Too many.'

'What's the plan?'

'Kill as many as we can. Hifa, when the next car starts, hit it with a grenade. We'll give cover. That way we'll get as many of them as have got over. Two cars have gone already.'

Maybe eight per car. Sixteen Others. The worst breach anywhere in a long time.

For the moment it was a standoff[2]. We couldn't get closer to them without coming out of cover and being easy to shoot. They couldn't get across the ramparts without being shot at.

'Where's the Captain?'

'Dead. He must be or he'd be here.'

But Sarge was wrong about that. A few seconds after he spoke, I heard a scrabbling and scratching noise behind me and to the left, the side furthest away from the barracks and the Others. The Captain came running up the nearest set of steps on the inside of the

1 bulwark: protective wall **2** standoff: *Pattsituation*

Wall and dived into cover beside us. He was bleeding from a cut on his head.

'Sir, we thought we'd lost you.'

'I was caught at the far end when they attacked,' he said, meaning he was past Hifa at the end of our section. I thought that I would have seen him go past but I took it on trust, since in a fight nothing much makes sense.

'We're going to wait here until the last of them have got over, then Hifa's going to light up their vehicle,' said Sarge. The Captain, panting, nodded.

'Good plan,' he said. He looked down for a moment. Then he stepped back and shot Sarge in the head, twice. He turned the gun towards the two Defenders who were standing nearest to the bench and shot them both with a burst, side to side. Yos dived to cover beside me. A hundred metres ahead of us I could see the Others all sprinting across the ramparts. They had been waiting for this moment. Hifa and I were on the far side of the bench, largely protected from the Captain, and that was what saved our lives, because he now turned to his left and started shooting at the Defenders who were under cover from the Others on the far side of the Wall, against the bulwark. I saw three of them go down and without thinking, without processing what I was doing – that training, when it kicks in, it really kicks in – I ran forwards and shoved my bayonet into his back. He staggered and fell and as he did I smashed him on the back of the head with the rifle. He went down and stayed down. Hifa stepped past the bench and took aim at the Others' vehicle, which was accelerating hard on the inner peripheral road. Her first grenade missed, short, but the second one didn't. The car exploded and swerved[1] off the road in flames. It was burning hard. No one would survive that.

I knelt down beside the Captain. Yos came over and joined me. We looked at each other but didn't speak. The Captain was unconscious and bleeding heavily. Maybe he'd survive, maybe not. I got

1 swerve (v): change direction suddenly

up and went over to Sarge. He had two bullet holes in the front of his face and the back of his head had gone. The two new people against the bench were both multiply wounded and were bleeding out. I went over to the Defenders next to the ramparts but as I was heading over I could hear engines and see lorries coming from both directions, from the next watchtowers to the east and to the west, and I knew that it was over. This part of it was over.

17

We were arrested. Nothing personal: when Others get over the Wall, that's what happens next. The Defenders from the neighbouring unit were the ones who had to execute the order, and they didn't seem happy about it, but the rules are what they are. We weren't handcuffed or anything, but the surviving members of our unit, all seven of us, were put in a lorry and driven south for about four hours, and then locked up in a barracks room which was like a normal barracks room except instead of small high windows there were no windows at all, the doors couldn't be opened from the inside, and we had to ask permission to go to the toilet. Yos wasn't able to whittle, because he wasn't allowed a knife, so he fidgeted non-stop.

We spent a month in that room. I got to know it so well I could recognise every crack in the ceiling. When it rained heavily there were damp patches and I got to recognise them too, to watch the changing shapes they made as the water seeped[1] in: map of small island, map of big island, map of continent; then back the other way when the rain stopped, shrinking, drying, gone. A parlour-game version[2] of the Change. The barracks room was standard, built to house thirty people, and there were only seven of us. It was me and Hifa and Hughes and Yos and three new Defenders who I barely knew. We spent most of our time talking about what had happened in the attack and trying to work it out. I imagine we were being listened to, but we didn't really care. It's not like we were expecting a reprieve[3]. We just wanted to try and make sense of it.

What was obvious was that the Captain had been working with the Others. They must have had other help too – lots of it. The talk of a network of supporters was true. Someone had cut the power,

1 seep in: flow in slowly **2** parlour-game version: miniature version **3** reprieve [rɪˈpriːv] (n): *Begnadigung*

someone had helped dynamite the barracks, someone had arranged the vehicles. Maybe somewhere else, somebody was getting them chipped, hacking into databases, faking IDs. It was hard to imagine how anybody could do that to us; but the truth was plain. While we Defenders were standing on the Wall, some of the people we were protecting were working to let Others over the Wall. It was like standing in front of a white-on-white painting and hearing the person next to you say that it was black-on-black. That's the main thing we talked about, the sense of betrayal we all felt. Hifa kept telling me to let it go, that people just did what they did and there was no explaining it, but I couldn't. I wanted to think about it, to try to understand it, but, at the same time, couldn't bear to. Betrayal by the Captain, betrayal by whoever it was that the Captain had been working with to help the Others. I had never really thought about betrayal before; I knew the word but not the meaning. Now I knew. Betrayal was like tasting a liquid, the bitterest thing you've ever put in your mouth, and holding the taste just long enough to fully understand how repulsive[1] it is, and then forcing yourself to drain the cup to the dregs[2].

Out of thirty Defenders in our company, only we seven in this barracks room had survived. We spent quite a lot of time trying to work out how many Others had got over the Wall and got away. Two people carriers' worth, was the general view. The third vehicle was fried by Hifa. Say eight to ten Others per vehicle. In the chaos and fighting, though, maybe the escape vehicles weren't full. Maybe one of the drivers had panicked, driven away with the car empty. It was tempting to imagine ... say, one car empty, only three people in the second car ... that would mean only three of us had to be put to sea. Or if the Others had been lucky and we had been unlucky, both cars had been full and twenty of them might have got over the Wall, so we'd all be going to sea. No way of knowing. But my hunch[3] was that those cars had been pretty full. A lot of Others had been seen running across the Wall.

1 repulsive: disgusting **2** dregs (pl): last drops **3** hunch: intuitive feeling

The extent of the conspiracy, the level of organisation, the planning and resources involved – it was hard to get my head around[1] it. If the breach had happened to a different company I would have been fascinated by the details. But you know what they say: when it's someone else, it's theory; when it's you, it's practice – and practice is very different from theory. And at the same time, the unique circumstances of our breach, the scale of the planning and the scale of the treachery, gave me moments when I did something stupid: I entertained a tiny hope. We talked it over and nobody could remember a breach that had involved people working with Others. Nothing like this – the breach, the assistance from within, the Captain's betrayal – had ever happened before. An extraordinary event would demand an extraordinary response. Mercy might be shown. Maybe. My head knew that this was very very unlikely, and that entertaining any hope would cost me dear when hope was taken away. But my heart couldn't stop itself. I wanted to be with Hifa, decades in the future, old people, much older than our parents were now, looking back at this terrible crisis from a safe happy afterlife, the moment when we nearly lost everything but were forgiven and brought back under the big safe all-embracing blanket of life behind the Wall. I couldn't resist the temptation of hope.

Every day or two I would be taken for interrogation. It happened to all of us in turn. The routine varied: armed Defenders would come and ask for us by name, or we'd be called to the door over the loudspeaker, or people would just come in, set up at one end of the room and start asking questions. The same questions, over and over, about what had happened that night, about what we had seen and what we had done. There were also questions about what had happened before, and questions about the Captain – lots and lots and lots of questions about the Captain. What did he do that night, where was he that night, where was he on previous nights, what had we noticed about him, what did he say, what did he usually do, what did he do that tour that was different, what did we think about him,

1 get your head around sth. (infml): understand sth.

on and on and on. Did he ever talk about his life away from the Wall, did he have friends on the Wall, what else did we know about him?

After four weeks we were put in a lorry again and driven to a town and put in cells – separate cells. There was a small high barred[1] window and a toilet in the corner of the room with a washbasin next to it. I spent a day and a night there. Then two Defenders came and led me into a room with a long table at one end. Five senior Defenders sat behind it. I was marched to the front of the room opposite them and asked if there was anything I wanted to say before I heard the sentence. I already knew there would be no trial, that wasn't the way it worked. That flicker of wishful thinking which I'd stupidly allowed myself did not survive standing in this room and looking at these pale solemn[2] closed faces. Hope is a mistake.

'Is there anything I can say that would make any difference?' I asked. They didn't seem to be expecting to be asked that and the officer in the middle, the senior one, looked from side to side and muttered something to his colleagues before turning his head back to me.

'No,' he said. I shrugged.

'Then, no,' I said, though I was tempted for a moment to say that I knew all the details of how the Others had done it, their secret network of supporters, just to see what would happen. I thought of something. 'One thing, though: how many of them got over the Wall?'

It was obviously irregular to ask questions, but the man in the middle thought it over for a few moments and decided to answer.

'We aren't sure but we think it was sixteen. Fifteen or sixteen.'

That made it the worst breach in many years. It would be untrue to say this made me feel better, because it was still a death sentence, but it did make me take it less personally. It was a huge thing that had happened and we had been caught up in. I nodded to show that I was ready for what was coming.

1 barred (adj): closed with bars **2** solemn: serious

'Joseph Kavanagh, you failed in your duty as a Defender, and you will be put to sea. May God have mercy on you,' said the senior Defender. 'Take him back to the cells.'

III

THE SEA

18

The third night at sea, I saw some lights in the far distance as we bobbed[1] up to the top of a swell. I wasn't sure I could believe my own eyes, the first time I caught a glimpse of them; your mind sometimes plays tricks on you when you're on the Wall, but on the open sea, it's worse. You have no physical equilibrium[2] in a small boat, and it can feel as if your mental equilibrium goes too. You can't trust your senses, and you can trust your imagination even less. You try to pin your mind down to the specifics of the moment. But it's hard. You hear things, you see things. The wind carried voices, fragments of song – not music in general, but specifically song, voices in chorus. I often thought I was hearing someone call my name. Clouds in the distance coalesced[3] as land, as hills, before fading back into cloud. So my first thought when I saw the lights was, I'm probably imagining it. I'm not used to a black this complete; on the Wall we had the lights along the guard posts. Here, until the moon comes up, it's blind-black. So maybe my synapses were firing weirdly, unused to a dark so final. Then, seconds later, on the crest[4] of another rise, I saw them again. And then, a minute or so later, a third time, more clearly and more definitely than before. Lights on the open sea.

We had talked about this: what to do, what calculations to make, if we saw evidence of other boats. The plan had been to row towards them and look for signs of whether they were benign[5] or not. By daylight that felt as if it made sense. At night, less so. We had no weapons and our only defence if we came under attack would be to try to get away as fast as possible. Given that we only had one set of oars[6], that wasn't very fast. A boat with lights was either a Coast

1 bob up: move upwards **2** equilibrium [ˌi:kwɪˈlɪbriəm]: balance **3** coalesce: gather **4** crest (n): highest part of a wave or a hill **5** benign [bɪˈnaɪn]: friendly, kind **6** oar: *Ruder*

Guard boat or a boat of Others so confident that they weren't worried about being seen. That meant that they were either stupid or well armed. Either was dangerous.

The swell was two metres or so, not enough to be frightening, but more than enough to be uncomfortable. It was the swell which made it hard to be certain about the lights; they winked into view at the top of each wave and then disappeared again as we went down into the trough[1]. Everyone else in the boat was asleep. It was a lifeboat, or it had been. A waterproof awning[2] covered the back half of the boat, and that's where the others were sleeping. It was also where our food supplies were stored. The water tanks and water catchment traps[3] were in the front of the boat, with me.

I wanted to wake someone up to talk about what we should do. Hifa would under normal circumstances have been the obvious choice, but she had been seasick for two days – not feeling-queasy[4] seasick, but repeatedly vomiting in a way which would be genuinely dangerous if it kept on – and had only just gone to sleep. It would not be the right call to wake her up. I chose Hughes. He was the only other person I trusted and he had done a little sailing with an uncle in his childhood, so he wasn't as ignorant about boats as I was. By which I mean: he knew almost nothing, but I knew nothing-nothing, so he won. It felt like a desperate thing to be doing, to rely on the tiny amount he knew about the sea, but there was no choice. I bent over double to get under the awning and into the back of the boat. You learnt the hard way to be careful when you did that, because if you brushed against the roof you were likely to get several litres of water decanted[5] onto you. I shoved Hughes with my foot, then again, and he woke up. I held my fingers to my lips. He sat up and crawled out of the sleeping space. There was just enough starlight to see that he looked terrible, his lips cracking with salt and his face abraded[6] red with the sea winds. I realised I must look like that too.

1 trough [trɒf]: *Wellental* **2** awning: big piece of cloth that is used as protection against sun or rain **3** water catchment trap: facility for collecting rainwater **4** queasy: feeling sick **5** decant: pour **6** abrade (fml): rub off

'This had better be good,' he said. I handed him a water bottle and pointed into the middle distance as we swayed up and down. He saw the lights as we got to the top of the second set of swells. He said nothing and looked at them for a while as they came in and out of view. I noticed he too was taking some time before he felt sure he could trust his senses.

'What I'm wondering is, if you think about who that might be, how many of the options are good for us?' I said.

He nodded. We stood at the prow[1] and looked into the distance while the boat bucked up and down on the swell and the lights winked on, winked off. Once I had had a few chances to study the lights I thought I could see they were arranged in a triangular pattern of five, one at the top and two lower down on each side.

'Same. Guards probably aren't out here at this time, but if they are and they see us, they'll sink us straight away, no question. So we can't go anywhere near them if they're Guards. If they're Others, how come they're making such a spectacle?'

A boat full of Others who felt confident enough to be fully illuminated on the sea in the middle of the night – to be that unfrightened, they would have to be very frightening.

'So we leave them be?'

He thought for a moment. It felt impossible that we would encounter the first sign of life out here, the first sign of company and possible salvation[2], and turn away from it. But when we thought about it, saw the risks, there was nothing else we could do.

'Plus, I think they're further away than they look. The horizon at sea level is about five K. The swell is coming from that direction. That's a lot of rowing into a lot of waves.'

'And only three of us to do the rowing.'

We looked at each other. We had been physically inactive for six weeks while we were waiting for sentence, and the rowing was hard. My hands were blistered[3] and split and I was getting out of breath

1 prow: front part of a ship **2** salvation: rescue **3** blistered: *mit Blasen bedeckt*

within minutes. Even if we wanted to row to the boat we might not be able to do it.

'OK. Thanks. Go back to sleep,' I said.

Hughes started to go back towards the covered part of the lifeboat. He stopped.

'In a few days we may be so desperate we have no choice,' he said.

'I know,' I said.

So this was life at sea. After the sentences were passed, we were taken in another lorry to another barracks. This time we travelled in handcuffs. I imagine the authorities' thinking was that we now had nothing to lose so were more likely to make a run for it[1]. That lorry journey was the worst moment of my life so far, worse than the moment of sentencing, worse even than when I knew the breach had happened and the Others had got away. I knew what the rules of the Wall were – like everyone else, I had known them my whole life. I don't remember having them explained to me because there was no time before the rules, before the facts of life: the sun comes up in the morning and goes down at night; if you throw something in the air, gravity makes it come back down; if the Others get over, you get put to sea. And yet, for all that, I felt sick with the injustice of it. Physically sick. I knew for certain that I, that we, had done nothing wrong. More: I had done everything I could to guard the Wall to the best of my capabilities. I had fought hard and watched my friends die. We all had. And this was our reward.

I had heard the word 'despair' and thought I knew what it meant; thought also that it was one of those states of mind that resembles a weather system, something which sets in and then you live with it or under it. Now I found that despair can also be something that happens to you, that it can hit you in a single moment. And then

1 make a run for it (infml): try to escape

it settles down with you for the duration. This is the thought I had in those days: that at some time in our lives we should, all of us, take some time to think about the worst possible thing that we can imagine happening to us. Your worst fear: track it down inside yourself. Take a good look at it. And face the fact that it will happen. The thing you dread most will happen. When it does, the name of the thing you're feeling is despair.

Our guards offered us the opportunity to write letters to our 'loved ones'. This wasn't a special dispensation[1]: it was clear that there was a protocol, agreed procedures, for occasions such as this. Agreed procedures for the worst thing that could ever happen to a person. In my case 'loved ones' meant my parents, and I decided I didn't want to write to them, because I had nothing to say. Hifa talked me out of that. I put down some platitudes about being sorry, even though I wasn't. I said I loved them, even though I didn't, at least not in that moment. But I felt better for having written the letter.

We stayed in that new barracks for several days and one by one were brought to the medical centre and put under general anaesthetic while we had our chips removed. No biometric ID, no life. Not in this country. No turning back ... After the operation we were held in recovery for a day, then returned to barracks. I could feel an itch deep in my arm where the chip had been and when I asked the others said they had the same feeling. A phantom chip. On the sixth afternoon, Hughes and Hifa and I were called and taken to another lorry; we'd have said goodbye to Yos and the other Defenders, if we'd known that was the last time we'd see them. From the angle of the light through the side of the vehicle I got the impression that we were heading south. We were driven until it was dark. Another barracks, but this time we were there hardly any time at all, an hour at most, before some Guards came into the room. From the look on their faces I could see this was what the Help had called *kuishia*: the ending. They seemed sad rather than angry; also implacable. We

1 dispensation: permission to do sth. that is usu. not allowed

were taken down a series of concrete tunnels and then suddenly were out in the open air, and a Guard ship was waiting, with a lifeboat tied to the side. As soon as I saw it I realised it was going to be ours. We were led across a gangway to the ship. The Guard captain was waiting for us and he, weirdly or generously, I'm still not sure which, maybe both, saluted us and shook our hands. The ship cast off and we headed out to sea and we were led downstairs to a small unfurnished cabin and the door was locked behind us.

Up to that point my despair had left me numb to other feelings. Despair, grief, numbness, blankness. But not much else. I felt there was nothing I could do, and as a corollary[1] (maybe) that there was therefore nothing else that it was necessary to feel. Everything that happened had been inevitable. Now and for the first time, I felt afraid, very very afraid. The boat would be lowered into the water and we would be lost, with the same complete lack of agency[2] we had had ever since the night of the attack. The feeling that I had been relying on to keep me numb – that there was nothing I could do – suddenly became a source of overmastering fear. There's nothing you can do. That thought can be a comfort, or it can be a terror. Panic, the need to flee, the impossibility of fleeing, the desperate need to escape combined with the certainty that you can't escape, the sense that you are going to die of dread right there in that moment. My heart was beating fast and erratically[3]. There was no air in the cabin. The lights had been turned up and were flickering. I was frying[4] in my clothes, where I'd felt cold only seconds before. Hifa saw me freaking out and put a hand on my arm. I flinched, as if I'd had an electric shock, then thought, why am I flinching, and that new idea was just enough, turned my attention just enough, to allow me to start slowing down.

'It's OK,' said Hifa, which was so not true it was a help. She wasn't looking at her best, pale and shaky, which turned out to be the start of her seasickness.

1 corollary: logical consequence **2** agency: ability to act **3** erratically: irregularly **4** fry (infml): (here) feel very hot

'Yeah, it's all great,' said Hughes.

'So great,' said Hifa. Her face was drawn. I could see that the attempt at banter between them was reflexive, a flashback to when we had been Defenders, when we had been on the Wall, and this was how we had talked to each other.

'I wonder how far they tow[1] us?' said Hughes, who got his answer straight away, because the engines slowed to an idle[2]. When people are put to sea, they are taken out of sight of land, so that they won't immediately try to turn and go back where they came from and also so that they won't run straight into Guard ships who would immediately sink them. We had been on the ship for about half an hour, so we couldn't be far from land. Say, fifteen K at most.

The door opened from the outside. Three Guards were standing there, with two behind them: the latter two were carrying guns. Again, they didn't look grim so much as sad. We came out and followed the unarmed ones down the corridor with the armed guards behind. They led us clanking up the ship's metal stairs out onto the main deck. It was relatively calm and still and the night was clear. They walked us over to the lifeboat, which was a couple of feet below the level of the deck, and we stepped across and down to get in. The whole crew came to the side of the ship and, on their captain's command, saluted as the lifeboat began to be lowered into the water. I swear that was almost the worst moment, the solemnity and finality of that salute.

The lifeboat swung a few feet further out as it was lowered and then, when we were just above sea level, was abruptly dropped into the water. We went crashing to the floor of the boat. When we'd got up and straightened ourselves out, the ship was moving away from us on a curving trajectory back towards land, alight like a floating cathedral in the pitch black[3] of the ocean. It was immediately clear how different the sea felt when you were centimetres above its sur-

1 tow (v): pull a boat by using a rope **2** idle (n): *Leerlauf* **3** pitch black: completely black

face on a pitching[1] small plastic boat, as opposed to a metal ship's deck ten metres high.

Having stood up, Hifa sat back down again. 'I'm not sure about this,' she said. It was my turn to be reassuring so I told her to sit where she was while Hughes and I sorted ourselves out. There were many boxes and crates[2] in the front of the boat, and we started to open them and look into them. The Guard had been generous, very generous, with supplies and assistance. We looked to have enough food for weeks. They had put in waterproof and warm clothing, torches and batteries and metal tools. There were several casks[3] of water too. I couldn't do the maths on that straight away, and I knew that people always needed more water than they thought they did; but it looked as if we would be able to survive for a while. As long as we weren't drowned or shot.

That, though, wasn't all the Guards had left us. We didn't go into the back part of the boat, under the awning, because the front was so full of food and equipment it needed to be reorganised before we could fight our way through. That made it confusing and weird when noises started coming from the back of the boat. Looking at each other wildly, Hifa and Hughes and I all simultaneously realised that we were not alone. Then a figure wrapped in a blanket came out of the back and straightened up. He was swathed[4] in multiple layers of cold-weather clothing and had a hood over his head and I thought I was hallucinating, or having an aneurysm[5], or something, because although I could recognise who it was I also couldn't get my brain to admit that I recognised him. The hair under the hood was blond. I know you but I don't know you, my brain was telling itself. Then he spoke and I saw that although I couldn't believe it, I had no choice.

'Hello,' said James the baby politician. 'I imagine you weren't expecting to see me.'

1 pitch (v): (here) move up and down on the water **2** crate: big wooden box **3** cask: wooden barrel **4** be swathed in sth.: be covered in sth. **5** aneurysm [ˈænjərɪzəm]: swollen artery (e.g. in the head)

Hifa and Hughes and I just stared at him. Their mouths were open and no doubt mine was too. James nodded and looked as pleased with himself as it is possible to look if you are huddled in a blanket on a lifeboat on the open sea. It wasn't comforting to see him, not at all, but I did feel momentarily less alone – as if it was a relief to find it wasn't just us Defenders who were put to sea.

'Yes, and there are other surprises in store. Come and look.'

Hifa got up and we moved towards the back of the boat, staggering and balancing on the boxes and gear as we went. The awning was folded down over both sides of the opening so we couldn't see in. James pulled it back and bent down and pointed. We crouched down to look. A person was lying on a foam mattress on the floor of the boat, wrapped in several layers of clothing and blankets. He was either unconscious or asleep. Despite the wrapping, we all recognised him at first glance. It was the Captain. James gave us a moment to take that in. 'So,' he said. 'Shall we kill him?'

19

I learnt that I had nearly killed him once already. The night of the attack, the Captain came close to bleeding out from the bayonet wound I'd given him. I'd hit an artery. If it had been up to us, his company, we would probably have let him die. But the medics got to him in time and he was stabilised and now, six weeks later, he was recovering, too weak to row but otherwise getting stronger. He did indeed look like a man who had nearly died; the skin on his face was stretched and the scars on his cheeks were now in parallel with newly drawn lines of illness and strain. His eyes were open and he stared at us and we stared back, but nobody spoke. It wasn't until the next morning that we talked to him.

That was a strange night, all crammed together in the back of the lifeboat. Three banished Defenders and their two companions. Companion number one was the member of the elite who had failed in his chance to stop what had happened. Companion number two was the man who had betrayed us. Sixteen Others had got over the Wall and escaped, and so sixteen people were put to sea. That was the seven members of the company who had survived and nine others in the chain of command, including several people in the next watchtowers along, who were judged to have reacted too slowly when the action kicked off that night. James said that the judgement had been passed on him because, according to the court, he should have realised that the Captain was part of the network of Others and their supporters. He thought that was outrageous[1]. He was bitter and did not pretend otherwise.

'My question is, how? How was I supposed to know?' My answer to that was that I didn't know and didn't care. I was glad that he felt

1 outrageous: scandalous, unacceptable

the injustice of what had been done to him as much as we felt the injustice of what had been done to us.

'A network of hidden support and I was meant to find one end of it and unravel[1] the network with what, the power of telepathy? I'm supposed to look into his soul and work out this plan they'd been hatching[2] for years?'

'How about you shut up?' Hughes said. James took the hint.

Hifa spent that first night retching[3], at first over the side, then into a bucket, then dry-retching where she lay. We lay there and I didn't feel as if I'd slept but I must have because I opened my eyes and the sun was some way above the horizon. Hughes and Hifa were standing at the front of the boat. The Captain was awake but silent under the awning. I woke James and went to the others and that's when we decided to have it all out and get the story. Hughes went under the awning and said something to the Captain and he got up and came to the bow.

The Captain sat with his back against the front of the lifeboat. We stood in front of him.

'It was ten years. Seven of us set out to get over the Wall. Then there were further expeditions with messages backwards and forwards. We had a set of signals with lights. I was the only one who made it. We all knew we would have to wait and in the end it was five years before I was able to get a message back. Then we moved to the next phase. I waited for three more years. Then I was a Captain and we could start to execute a specific plan. By now we had got in touch with a wider network. Some of your countrymen don't agree with the Wall. They think you need the Wall to keep out the water but not to keep out human beings. Some of them don't agree with turning people into Help. They think it's slavery. It's a big network, much bigger than you realise. I don't know much about who is in it and I don't know who they're helping but I do know that my people are not the only ones who are coming.'

1 unravel sth.: disclose sth., clear up sth. **2** hatch (v): *ausbrüten, aushecken*
3 retch: make sounds as if vomiting

He stopped. We wanted something more and I could tell that he knew it. The silence went on – the human silence, because the wind and waves and creaking of the boat never stopped. It is never silent in a small boat in northern waters. Eventually it was Hifa who spoke. Her voice was hoarse from her hours of retching.

'Aren't you going to say you're sorry?'

The Captain was stiff and still, leaning back rigidly, and I felt there was a strong reaction he wanted to give but wouldn't. He thought for a long time.

'The thing we most despise about you, you people, is your hypocrisy[1]. You push children off a life raft[2] and wish to feel good about yourselves for doing it. OK, fine, if that's what you want to do, but you can't expect the people you push off the side of the raft to think the same. To admire your virtue and principle while we drown. So, no, I'm not going to be like you. I'm not going to lie, I'm not going to be a hypocrite, and I'm not going to say I'm sorry.'

'Not even for Sarge?' said Hifa.

He blinked but said nothing. In that moment I did want to kill him. I looked over at Hifa, who mainly seemed as if she was going to be sick again, and at James, who was standing with his lips pursed shaking his head, looking like someone on a television debate panel[3] trying to make it clear to the audience that he disagreed with an argument being made by a fellow panellist. Then I looked over at Hughes, and what I saw on his face was the look of a man who was in the middle of suffering a huge, all-encompassing[4] disappointment. My anger subsided and began to turn into a sense of loss. I felt sad. Loss, loss, there was just so much loss, in what had happened to us, in what the Captain had done, in what we had done to the world, in what we had done to each other and in what was happening to us.

'Let's kill him,' said James. If he had said that same thing five minutes before, and if I had had a gun or knife in my hand, I would probably have done it then and there. But a couple of minutes can

1 hypocrisy: *Heuchelei, Scheinheiligkeit* **2** life raft: *Rettungsfloß* **3** panel: group of participants in a public discussion **4** all-encompassing: total

have a big effect on how you see things, and the moment for revenge had, for me, passed. We were probably all going to die anyway, and in this boat. Sending the Captain on ahead of us didn't seem like it was worth doing.

'Yes, you could do that,' the Captain said. 'Or you could let me lead you to somewhere safe.'

Safe. I wouldn't have thought it possible for a single word to have such an impact. Safe. To think of being safe meant to have hope, and I knew, had learnt recently, how dangerous hope is. And yet, out here on the sea, we couldn't live without it. The Captain's plan was to head south. He said there were islands and stretches of coast where we could find somewhere to stay. He said we would never be able to get back over the Wall but there were other places to live. He said he was the only one among us to have made a long journey in a boat and he knew how to do it and he could do it again. He said because we came from an island we thought the whole world had a wall around it, but that wasn't true and there were places, not many but some, where we could get to safety. More safety than we would have at sea, anyway. He said again that the important thing was to head south. He said that apart from anything else, the cold here in the north was dangerous and once we got thoroughly wet, as we would when there was bad weather or when the season changed, it would become more dangerous still.

'If we get drenched[1], we may never dry out. If the boat floods, we die. If we capsize[2], we die. This is not the Wall. We can't go back to barracks to dry out. We have to go south.'

Then he went and sat in the back of the boat while we sat at the front and discussed it. When he moved, especially when he got up or changed position, you could see the effect of his wound was still strongly present. The wind and waves were now getting stronger. Every deeper plunge[3] brought a slap of salt spray into the boat.

'South,' said Hughes.

1 drench sb./sth.: make sb./sth. thoroughly wet **2** capsize: turn over **3** plunge (n): fall, dive

'We have no reason to trust him,' said James. 'We have less reason to trust him than any human being alive.'

'We have so little reason to trust him that we have no reason not to trust him,' said Hughes. I thought that I knew what he meant: the Captain would know he had so little credibility with us that there was no incentive[1] to lie. Also, the unspeakable truth was I still felt an instinct to trust him and be led by him. He just so obviously was a leader. At the same time I felt that instinct was craven[2] and doglike. Follow master, follow, off the edge of the cliff, not once but twice.

'South,' said Hifa. It sounded like a tentative[3] conclusion, a provisional verdict. What else, after all, was there to do? Rely on Hughes's experience sailing with his uncle, mainly on a big pond near his house but twice in a river estuary on family holidays?

'South,' I said. So we had taken the Captain's advice. There was a compass among the survival kit that we had been left by the Guards. And now here we were, bobbing up and down on a two-metre swell, hiding from lights in the dark. Hughes and I stood looking at them for a few minutes longer and then he patted me on the arm and went back towards the awning at the back of the boat.

I let Hughes duck under the cover and began pulling at the oars to move us in the opposite direction, away from the ship and its lights. We took rowing easy, because it was hard work, especially for the unfit, and because doing it too energetically made you perilously[4] hungry. It was a trade-off, calories for movement. I was rowing backwards so, when the waves permitted, I could see the lights in the distance. The ship didn't seem to be growing any further distant; then, slowly, it seemed that it was. I must have rowed for an hour, with frequent breaks at the start, and then with longer periods of rest than bursts of rowing. I was using the same technique we used to employ on the Wall, spacing out glances at my watch to try and make it a pleasant surprise when I gave in and looked at the time. When my four-hour shift was over I went to wake James for

1 incentive: motivation **2** craven: *feige* **3** tentative ['tentətɪv]: provisional
4 perilously: dangerously

his turn. In the back of the boat, Hifa and the Captain and Hughes were all deeply asleep, and so was James until I shook him. I stood back to let him wake in his own time.

He got up slowly, rubbing not just his eyes but his whole face, making chewing movements with his mouth. Then he came out from under the awning.

'I saw lights,' I told him. 'A few kilometres away. A ship. Hughes saw them too. We talked it over and decided to leave it. Too late to do anything about it now. I wanted you to know.'

He nodded, thinking about it. I didn't trust him but he wasn't stupid. I could see him running through the same calculations we had made.

'OK,' he said. 'I'd have done the same.' He nodded some more. It was beginning to be light, and I could see how tired he was, but how determined too. Fatigue and his blond stubble made him look ten years older than he had before we were banished. I went to climb into the back and take my turn sleeping, but he stopped me with a hand on my arm. I looked a question at him and he held up a finger. Then he rummaged[1] under his layers of clothing, the layers he never took off except when he had to lower his trousers to defecate over the side of the boat. He wriggled for a moment and then brought something out, as if it were a birthday present. It was an object about six inches high with a circumference about the same size. It took me a few seconds to believe my own eyes, though I knew very well what it was: a high-explosive grenade.

'Jesus, James,' I said. He was smiling.

'The commander of the Guard ship gave it to me,' he said. 'In case we run into trouble or in case we, you know, decide we can't go on any more. In case we want to choose fire over water.'

I looked at him hard and saw something I had never seen before, never even suspected, which was the glint of madness. I said:

'You can't possibly be—' but he cut me off.

1 rummage: *durchwühlen, durchstöbern*

'I'm not, I'm not,' he said. 'I just wanted you to know.' He began putting the grenade back under his clothes. I wasn't worried about it going off by accident, that was impossible with the design of those grenades; in fact it was hard enough getting them to detonate when you wanted them to. What I was worried about, though, was his state of mind. I decided I would tell Hifa and Hughes about the grenade – the next time I could be with them privately.

I went and lay down and replayed what had happened, not with James, but earlier, with the lights in the distance. Through the next days, through all that happened, I found myself often thinking of those lights; wondering who they were, what boat they had been on, Guards or Others, or Defenders put to sea, even, perhaps, sea ships going about their business, carrying precious cargo or passengers who knew where. I couldn't get it out of my mind. All kinds of alternative futures bloomed into being when I thought about that boat, who had been on it, where they might have taken us. Friendly brigands[1], who would have made us part of their crew. Pitying Guards, with the convenient ability to issue us with new chips and fake IDs. Or, more likely, merciless pirates who would have robbed and killed us on sight. I'd never know. In my old life, if I had wanted to find something out sufficiently badly, I could. I would put my mind to it, devote resources to it, find an answer. That was no longer true. There were now many things that I would never know and never be able to find out.

On the fourth day we had our first piece of luck. (Always bearing in mind Sarge's maxim that if we had truly been lucky we would never have been there in the first place.) Hifa's seasickness had ended, thank God, as abruptly as it had begun, on the third day. She was washed out and her cheekbones were sharper and her nose pointy under her cap. She looked, if I had to put it in one word, purposeful.

It was mid-morning and she was on watch. I was sitting in the front of the boat because the air in the back would sometimes get

1 brigand ['brɪgənd]: bandit, robber

stuffy. When the weather was dry and the pitching of the boat not too severe, it could actually be quite pleasant to sit in front, in the intervals when you weren't consumed with anxiety and apprehension and plain terror. Hifa was standing at the tiller[1] looking forwards and Hughes was rowing, slowly, taking long pauses between strokes. Hifa was looking very fixedly at the horizon.

'Can you come and hold this for a minute?' she said to me. I took the tiller. Hifa came right to the front of the boat and stood staring into the distance.

'Right,' she said, 'I'm sure. There is land in front of us and about fifteen degrees to the left. At first I thought I was imagining it but I'm definitely not. It's an island.'

Hughes stopped rowing, I let go of the tiller and we both joined Hifa at the front of the boat. My first thought was: she's wrong. There was a short smudgy[2] line on the horizon but the thing it most looked like was a bank of cloud. One of those mirages[3], those imagined solid shapes which were so tormenting at sea. I stood and looked a bit more. I took off my glasses, thought about wiping them, thought better of it and put them back on. Actually, maybe ...

'It's land,' said Hughes, and hugged Hifa. They did a clumsy little jig[4]. I still wasn't sure. My desperate wish to believe them made me reluctant to believe them. I kept looking. The line did not move or wave or blur as clouds tended to. I kept looking. Almost with reluctance, I gave in to hope and admitted to myself: yes, it was land. Land!

Hughes and I went back to the oars and took one each. We started to row in the direction of the land. There was no immediate way of guessing its distance, since high ground would be visible from much further away than low; it could be thirty kilometres, it could be as little as three to five. My guess was that it was low land

1 tiller: handle for steering small boats **2** smudgy: with unclear edges
3 mirage ['mɪrɑːʒ]: illusion **4** jig (n): short dance

and not too far. My reasoning was that high ground might accumulate its own weather, wisps[1] of cloud above the highest point.

The wind was from the side and the boat rocked and bumped as we headed towards the miracle of land. Sometimes the oars would catch too deep, sometimes they would miss altogether. It made rowing even harder work than usual. Since we were put to sea blisters had formed on my hands, then burst, and the raw skin underneath was acutely painful. We took the oars for half an hour at a time, Hifa and James joining in. The Captain came out of the back of the boat to watch.

All I could think of was how easy it would have been to miss the island altogether. It was pure luck. In the night we would have gone straight by without the merest inkling[2] of its presence. So much of our new life was about luck.

We rowed for a couple of hours and the island was close now, a few hundred metres away. The next problem became clear to all of us at the same time. I looked at Hifa and Hughes and James and they looked back at me. The Captain was standing right at the front of the lifeboat.

'No no no,' said Hughes.

It was easy to see what he meant. There was nowhere to land. The island – beachless, like every coastline in the world after the Change – rose vertically out of the sea. All that was left of the low island it had formerly been was the upper part of its main hill. Or rather, hills, three of them, a triple-peaked mass. The three slopes were bare rock. The wind and waves smashed into them and if we went in too close, we would be smashed against them too. Even on a sunny, calm day, with a powerful ship able to hold its own[3] against the winds and currents, it didn't look as if it would be possible to get a foothold, not on this side of the island. In our boat and with our resources we would have no chance.

The Captain turned around.

1 wisp: thin line **2** inkling: intuitive knowledge **3** hold one's own: *sich behaupten*

'This isn't the only possible angle of approach,' he said. That made sense. We would pull back, give it some space, take a tour around the island and see if there was anywhere we could land. Hifa turned the boat to the side and I stepped away from the oars to let James go solo. There was no rush now; we'd take as long as we needed. This might be our best chance of medium-term survival and we didn't want to skip past it in any hurry. At the same time, I felt a deep, almost nauseous[1] sense of dread. My gut[2] was telling me that there would be nothing to look at. The island was too steep, too rocky, a cliff in the middle of the ocean; I desperately wanted there to be a landing point, but I couldn't imagine what it would look like. The rowing was hard, even harder than it had been before, and as we turned to manoeuvre around the island the waves came from all points of the compass so that the boat bucked and rocked more wildly than ever. This is impossible, I thought, we will never be able to land here.

I was half right. As we went around it became clear that the island was variations on a theme: vertical stone. It wasn't just unsafe to land, it was unsafe to get too close. A shipwreckers' dream of an island. And yet I was half wrong too, because as we came round into the lee of the island, hidden from the wind, in the sudden still and quiet, I saw the first good thing I had seen since we were put to sea: a flotilla of boats, floating together in the unexpected calm.

1 nauseous: making you feel as if you are about to vomit **2** gut: *(hier) Bauchgefühl*

20

The strangest thing about the next few days was how quickly we got used to our new life. I tried to keep a low profile[1] and set myself the task of finding out what this all was, what it meant – who these people were and how they had got here. The floating community had ten members, before we arrived. They had eight sea-going vessels[2] tied together and a couple of floating structures which were not seaworthy, not in any kind of weather, but were float-worthy. The community had not been a plan, more a series of accidents and coincidences. The first three boats had arrived in the lee of the island before the last winter began and had taken shelter, and then had found that the supply of protein (fish) and water (rain) could sustain them, and had stayed. The other boats – the other Others – had arrived piecemeal[3] and over time. Their crews were from nowhere and anywhere. I'd been brought up not to think about the Others in terms of where they came from or who they were, to ignore all that – they were just Others. But maybe, now that I was one of them, they weren't Others any more? If I was an Other and they were Others perhaps none of us were Others but instead we were a new Us. It was confusing.

Members of the floating community couldn't go ashore, but they, we, were safe in the calm. It was nobody's idea of an ideal life but it was a life that could be lived. Traps, catchments and lines were all over the floating craft, in their hundreds: for food, I saw to my amazement, they were quite well supplied. The big lack was in fuel: there were only tiny quantities of wood, which was too precious to burn, and an equally tiny quantity of diesel fuel brought by one of

1 keep a low profile: avoid people's attention **2** sea-going vessel: boat capable of navigating the ocean **3** piecemeal: individually, bit by bit

the boats. It wasn't clear what to do with that so it was being kept for emergencies.

The second day after our arrival, I was walking around the rafts trying to understand how it all worked and I came to the side of the community furthest from the sunken island. This was the biggest of all the rafts. A woman with wild black and grey hair was squatting[1] as she wrestled with something I couldn't see clearly but which was still alive and fighting.

'I'm not going to pretend that looks good,' I said. The woman laughed. The sea life made it difficult to tell how old people were but she was maybe in her mid-forties, strong-looking and intent on her work. I now had a better view of what she was doing. She had trapped a seagull in a net; she broke its neck with a single expert wring. You could see she had done this many times before. The bird went limp and the woman's shoulders dropped with relief. She gestured at me to sit so I did.

'What's the worst thing you ever ate in your life?' she said, half smiling, as she started to pull feathers off the bird. She spoke good English with a lilt[2], an accent from somewhere far away and a rhythm which had something not-English underneath it.

'You mean, before I got here?'

She laughed at that too.

'I don't really remember,' I said. On the Wall, thinking about food had been a means of escape, a technique for casting your imagination into the future, into a time when you weren't on the Wall any more. At sea, thinking about food had become a form of nostalgia, of time travel back to a safer place. On the Wall, thinking about food made you feel better. Out here, it made you feel worse. 'To be honest, looking back, it all seems pretty good now. I had some stews and things I thought were impossible to eat but I'd give anything to have them today.'

1 squat (v): *sich hinhocken* **2** lilt: *Tonfall*

'Whatever it was, gull is nastier. Believe it. A rank taste and a bitter taste. As bad as you can imagine. Game bird[1] and fish. At the same time. Tough too. Juice runs when you sink your teeth in. Blood, salt, duck, fish oil. Hard to swallow. And that's if you cook it. We can't use fire so we have to eat it raw. That's so much worse. Trick is to leave it to dry. It's still hard to chew but the flavour changes. You can get it down without gagging[2]. Like jerky[3] or pemmican[4]. Fish-duck jerky. We store it for when we're low on protein. No choice.'

No choice. That made sense. It was true for most things on the sea. Her boat – it seemed to be hers, though the sense of ownership might be a function[5] of her strength of personality rather than anything more formal – was a large improvised raft made of wood. There were nets strung in the air all around the boat to catch birds, and lines hanging off it all around in the water to catch fish. Rainwater catchment vessels were dotted all over the vessel. Including me, there were six or seven people on this raft, two of them solemn children who had been given, or had given themselves, the job of finishing off any birds or fish brought into the boat: they carried clublike sticks with a thickened metal piece on the end. The children took sidelong glances at me when they thought I wouldn't notice. It was as if I too was a form of non-human life which might at any moment need to be whacked[6] on the head. Killed and eaten too, maybe. Did children have thoughts like that? Or was imaginative darkness of that sort an adult thing? I didn't know enough about them to know. The next time I caught the boy peeking at me I smiled and winked back. He quickly looked away.

Beyond the children were three girls, older than the children but not old enough to count as adults. I never saw them more than a stride[7] or two away from each other. They spent most of their time whispering to each other, conspiring or sharing secrets. It was

1 game birds: bigger birds that are hunted and eaten **2** gag (v): have the feeling you are going to vomit while eating sth. **3** jerky: dried meat **4** pemmican: food made from crushed dried meat **5** be a function of sth.: depend on sth. **6** whack sb./sth. (infml): beat sb./sth. **7** stride (n): long step

hard to know what those secrets would be, in a place like this; but maybe that made having them all the more important. They were not sisters – their ethnicities were visibly different – but they spoke a shared language which was not English. The shortest and most confident of them acted as their spokesperson and interlocutor[1]. The girls were slowly and desultorily[2] lifting fishing lines out of the water and checking them. They had the air of teenagers who are pretending to be busy in order to prevent adults from giving them something more demanding to do.

'I'm Mara,' the woman said, as she kept plucking the seagull. 'I'm married to him.' She pointed across to a man who was moving towards us, the same age as her, also wiry, also tough, his beard scissors-clipped and orderly. The floating people had their own technique for crossing the ropes and nets between the rafts: instead of slowing down and picking their way carefully, they sped up and put their feet so precisely on the knots and firmer planks that they seemed to skip[3] over the water. This man was so confident on the tricky passage between rafts that he was brisk and delicate, like a goat on a steep hillside. Once he was on the big raft he had a few words with the teenagers then a few words with the children, and then he came to Mara and me and squatted down in front of us.

'I'm Kellan,' he said. He had the same up-and-down, not-quite-English lilt as his partner. Kellan didn't say he was in charge; he didn't have to. I knew already that there were people here who knew a lot about how to live at sea, and it was clear that I had now met two of them. I got the story later. Kellan and Mara had been raised by two sets of parents who were keen sailors before the Change; they met at sea, across on the far side of the Atlantic; they more or less grew up on boats. You felt that the closer you stayed to them, the better your chances of keeping alive.

'I'm Kavanagh,' I said. He nodded and looked at me. Not friendly and not unfriendly, but assessing. 'I'm grateful to you for taking us

1 interlocutor: person taking part in a conversation **2** desultory: without enthusiasm **3** skip: jump

in,' I said, partly because it was true and partly because I felt the need to say something.

'We voted,' he said. It wasn't clear which way he'd voted, but Mara was smiling at me.

'OK,' I said. 'Well, thank you for that. Thank you for what you did.' It didn't seem close to adequate, but then what can you say to people who have taken you in and saved you from certain death? 'Thank you for what you did.' We had not told them who we were, that we were Defenders who had been put to sea. It seemed certain that it would not improve our chances of being given sanctuary[1] if they knew that our entire life's purpose had been to stop people like them getting to safety.

He let the silence lengthen for a moment or two and then Mara laughed.

'Don't let him tease you, we all agreed. We wanted some more people who can look after themselves.'

Kellan was smiling too now. He said, 'You look like a swimmer.'

I said that I was, a bit. Swimming wasn't especially popular in the world after the Change, but it had been my best sport at school. Nobody swam in the sea any more.

'The water here isn't deep,' he said. 'Not hard to see why, the sea floor underneath us used to be part of this island. The one we can look at but can't touch.'

We stood for a moment and looked at the island and I imagined what it had once been like – beaches, gentle slopes, maybe a few houses down near the water. In living memory the sea floor below us was dry land. All drowned now. Part of the old drowned world.

'When the water isn't turbulent we can see the sea bed. It's only a few metres down. Less in some places. We reckon there's probably things down there we can eat. Sea vegetables, shellfish, who knows. Perhaps there are techniques we could use to catch fish further down, not just lines off the side of the rafts. A person with good lungs could dive to the sea bottom. Strong boy like you, maybe you

1 sanctuary: shelter, safe place

can go down and take a look. Not all at once, have a few goes, build your fitness up. As long as you can see down there?'

He made a gesture in the direction of my eyes, or rather my glasses.

'No, that's fine,' I said. 'It's different under water. I can see OK. Swimming makes you hungry, though. I could easily end up burning and eating more calories than I find.'

He shrugged.

'The only way we'll work it out is by giving it a try. I'm more worried about the cold. Worried on your behalf. That's why I want to do it now. Later in the year, when the season turns, it'll be too late. Too much of a risk to try it. Now, if you keep it short and sweet, the chance is worth it. Or at least I think so, but it's you going into the water. So you must think it through for yourself.'

'I'll try it,' I said. It would of course have been difficult to say no to the person responsible for giving us sanctuary; Kellan was well aware of that. His way of leading was different from the Captain's, but it was effective.

'Good,' he said. Then he looked at Mara tearing up her gull and said, 'I think I'll leave you two to it.'

'Get stuffed[1], old man,' said Mara. Kellan laughed and went over to the children, who made play-fighting moves as he approached, and then went to talk to the teenagers. I noticed that when they realised he was coming over to them they became much more busy around the fishing lines.

That was how I got the job of being the community's diver. I was glad of having something specific to do. Hifa was given the job of experimenting with bird traps, Hughes was to join me in trying to dive, James and the Captain were put on a mixture of watch and fishing duties. Nobody was idle[2]. There were always things to do concerning traps and nets and food preparation. I could see the talent Kellan and Mara had for the work of survival, not just because

1 be stuffed (infml): have a full stomach after eating a lot of food **2** idle (adj): lazy, doing nothing

diving was an idea worth trying but because it gave my days a sense of purpose and structure and something to do other than just exist and wait for … for … it wasn't clear what. If we were to leave, the sensible thing would be to get on with it. The sun still had some warmth, but the days were getting shorter and the year would soon turn. Winter would be a difficult time to travel, so if we were going to head south, we would need to leave before long. To gather our strength and head off. I tried to think about that and found that I couldn't bear to. Winter would also be a difficult time to stay on the water, on the rafts, but the community had already survived a winter and knew how to do it. I could almost hear a voice whispering 'stay, stay …' The truth was, it was hard to imagine ever getting away from here. But it might be that we would never need to. Perhaps we weren't waiting for anything, but this was just life, life in its new form. There had been floating communities before, in the world before the Change. So maybe that is what we now were and would always be. It was better not to brood on it, so I tried not to. I tried to stick to the daily necessities.

My diving work started that same day, as soon as Kellan left us. I took a long look over the side of the raft at the spot where Mara was plucking her seagull. It was unpromising. I couldn't see the sea bed. I walked around the rafts looking for places where the water seemed shallowest. I hadn't even begun mastering the art of moving around on the rafts. On a boat, everything moves in a coordinated way, so even when you are bucking and dropping and swaying on the waves, there's a kind of logic and coherence to the fact that you're on a single platform. The boat dips and swings left, you dip and swing with it. The dancing of the rafts was much more complicated and involved many moving parts jigging to subtly different rhythms. I found myself staggering and tripping even when the water was relatively still. My frequent trips and falls were painful and disconcerting and they were made more irritating by the sight of Hifa moving light-footedly and rapidly across the rafts as she checked the fishing lines. She had got the hang of it straight away.

Hughes joined me and we kept walking around the community trying to find a place for our first dive. We took turns: one of us would hold onto the other as he leant as far as possible over the side, face just above the water. We could always have started by diving in and seeing the underwater conditions first-hand and for ourselves, but the water was cold and I thought our stamina[1] would give out. We'd manage one or two dives and then have to stop. Better to do some research first. The sea was a little turbulent that day and although the anchors gave evidence that the water was only a few metres deep, we couldn't see the bottom, which was discouraging. Neither of us liked the idea of making our first plunge down into murk[2] where we had no visibility. It's a primal fear, the idea of the thing lurking[3] below you in the deep. We wanted to dive where we could see. The trouble was there didn't seem to be any clear water anywhere around the rafts. I started to think we would have no choice but to go to wherever was shallowest, according to the anchors, and dive to the bottom to take a chance on what was down there. But then our luck changed. We found a spot which looked as if it might be viable[4]. It was on the innermost, island side of the rafts. The water was slightly shallower, and clear enough to see the bottom, which had patches[5] of bare brown and patches of green. It might not have been more than ten or twelve feet, easily diveable.

I didn't relish[6] the thought of the cold, but the water, at this point where it was clear, looked cleansing and elemental and inviting. I wanted to have the first try at diving and said so.

'Be my guest,' said Hughes. We got some spare cloth to use as a towel and borrowed a metallic space blanket; I knew that once I got out of the water I would be desperate to dry off and warm up as quickly as I could. With no external sources of heat, I would be using my own body warmth, what was left of it. Fine. But best be prepared. I stripped off and put my foot in the water and then realised that

1 stamina: strength that enables you to keep on doing sth. for long periods of time **2** murk: darkness **3** lurk (v): lie in wait **4** viable: manageable **5** patch (n): small area of sth. **6** relish sth.: enjoy sth.

this was one of those times when there's no point taking too long to get yourself ready, so I let myself go all the way in. The cold was shocking and, for a moment, obliterating[1]: I had no thoughts, only the sensation of complete, stinging, icy cold. I came back up to the surface spluttering[2] and coughing. Hughes, leaning down close to the side of the raft, looked worried. No doubt that was partly concern for me and partly the thought that it was going to be his turn next.

'Five minutes,' I said when I had got my breath. 'Tell me.' He nodded. I emptied my lungs, breathed deeply, exhaled completely, refilled them, and dived.

The cold was stinging but it was thrilling to be in the water, that sensation of flying downwards. I felt free, unburdened. In a few seconds I was at the bottom. The sea bed was covered in a thick mat of what appeared to be grass from the surface, but up close you could see it was two different kinds of seaweed, one long and frond-like[3], the other mossy and dense. I took a handful of each, having to pull a little harder than I expected, and once I felt my breath starting to give out, went back to the top. I gave the seaweed to Hughes, caught my breath and dived again. It would be a good idea to take a knife down next time, because the frond-like grass grew two or three feet tall and it was easy to imagine it wrapping around your legs when you tried to head back to the air. I brought up several more handfuls of the different seaweeds. On my fourth and final dive, I found something hidden in between the moss and the grass, a shell, and snatched at it, again pulling harder than I thought I'd have to. A scallop[4]. I pushed back up to the surface with a sense of elation[5] but when I got there, I was too weak to pull myself out of the water. Hughes had to help me. He wrapped me first in the improvised towels, then in the space blanket. After a minute, as I warmed up, I started shivering. That made me realise I had pushed my body tem-

1 obliterate sth.: completely destroy sth. **2** splutter (v): produce explosive short sounds **3** frond-like: leave-like **4** scallop: shellfish that can be eaten
5 elation: great happiness

perature dangerously low: when you are too cold to shiver, you're on the edge of full-blown hypothermia. That was a lesson I had learned during type 2 cold on the Wall. Out here that degree of cold would almost certainly kill you.

Kellan came over while I was recovering and Hughes was psyching[1] himself up for his turn. He picked over the seaweed and tapped the scallop. He looked pleased.

'I don't know if any of this is edible,' I said.

'All seaweed is edible,' said Kellan. 'This is good, very good. Vitamins are not easy here. So this is a real help. Also where there's one scallop there will be others and they're just over a calorie per gram.'

'I don't know how many turns we can do at a time. It's just too cold.'

'We'll get a rota[2] going once we work out what's down there and where it is. You should only do one set of dives each per day. You can be in charge. Good, well done, Kavanagh.' He reached out and, a paternal gesture that seems strange to describe but at the time felt right, ruffled my hair.

Hughes did only three dives and at the end of them he was shivering – cold, but not as cold as I had been. We set three dives as a daily maximum. Over the next week or so Hughes and I mapped the sea bed around the community and, where it was safe, underneath the rafts. Once we grew more confident we started exploring the areas where we couldn't see the bottom from the raft. It was anxious work the first couple of times, diving where you couldn't see. My particular fear was that while I was under water I would drift sideways and get below the floating structures, become disoriented, then try to come to the surface and be trapped. I realised though that while you couldn't see clearly to the surface, there was always light, so you always knew which way was up. It was not hard to detect where the rafts were. It was dangerous but not complicated. We found a great deal of seaweed, enough to make it clear that there

1 psych yourself up: mentally prepare yourself for sth. unpleasant **2** rota: work plan

was what amounted to an infinite supply. That was good news, not least because the seaweed tasted pretty good, once you gave it a quick rinse in rainwater to get the salt off: it was fresh and sharp and green and I found I could visualise it doing me good on the inside, charging up my supply of nutrients[1] and vitamins.

In addition to all the seaweed we found three areas with a good quantity of scallops. These were frustrating, because the shells were beautiful and big, broader than an outstretched palm, but then when you opened them the shellfish was nothing but a dab[2] of red coral and a coin-sized blob of meat. The rule sometimes seemed that the bigger and more promising the shell, the smaller the yield of edible scallop. The fact that they were delicious, tangy[3] and sweet and subtle, was a cruel trick; such hard work to get them, but so small, but so good ... They were excellent for morale, though, especially with the new supply of seaweed to vary the diet of seabirds and mackerel[4].

Kellan had been waiting for a while to investigate the sea bed, but hadn't done so because there was nobody able to do it. We could tell that there had once been more people in the floating community. The subject was never discussed. If enough time went past, I was planning to ask what had happened to the rest of them; to ask in detail, I mean, because I could guess the rough outline. They had sailed away looking for some solid ground and had not come back. Perhaps some of them had succeeded in getting to land in the south. It wasn't impossible. It was also possible some of them had died trying to get over the Wall. I didn't want to think about that too much.

James did some diving too, but he was a poor swimmer and wasn't fit, so he didn't bring up much of anything. Hifa was better but she got cold quickly and she was doing such good work with the fishing that it was a more effective use of her time. As for the Captain, he wasn't well enough yet to swim let alone to dive, so he spent most of the day working on the nets, repairing them. He sat

1 nutrient: *Nährstoff* **2** dab (n): small amount **3** tangy: tasty **4** mackerel: *Makrele*

on a plastic crate on the side of the raft and picked over the lines and nets. When he saw a weak spot he set to the task of stitching and sewing it back together: an incongruous sight but somehow an ancient one too, the fisherman fixing his tools. The children were frightened of him at the start but after a few days began going over to sit beside him and watch him work. They were fascinated by his facial scars. I once saw him sitting on his plastic crate while two of them, standing in front of him, reached out and touched them, very carefully, as if he might suddenly change his mind and leap up at them. It occurred to me that he was the only one of us who had left children behind. I had no feelings about that: his choices were what they were. The teenage girls sometimes went over too and sat with him; he had a language in common with one of them. I could occasionally hear the two of them laugh together. He gave them small jobs testing the repaired lines or feeling over the nets to look for weak spots for him to inspect.

In general I avoided the Captain. Since we had been put to sea, since the time he had said why he had done what he did, I don't think I had heard him utter twenty sentences. He was as quiet in the community as he had been on the lifeboat, and it was hard to know what he thought. I found it difficult to believe that he would prefer being on the open sea to being here, though. One day we went diving near the section of raft where he was mending his nets, and when I came up I was only a few feet away from him. I dried myself and wrapped myself in the space blanket and shivered myself back to warmth. Hughes went to get some dried fish from Mara's big raft. I stood hopping and jiggling. He was passing a net through his hands, looking for holes and damage. He did not look at me. But I had something I wanted to know.

'Do you ever think about it? What they would do if they knew who we are?' I said to him. I think the subtext[1] of that was: do you,

1 subtext: hidden meaning

an expert in deception for many years, feel any remorse[1] about this new deceit?

'They do know. I told them,' he said.

I should have been used to being surprised by what the Captain did, but that proved I still didn't have the measure of him. I stopped still.

'You could have got us all killed. More likely than not.'

He shrugged. 'No more lies.'

'Your lies.'

'Everybody's lies.'

I thought about it for a moment.

'What did they say?'

'They told me that they have a saying here: nothing before the sea was real.'

This conversation with the Captain was one I replayed over and over afterwards. I thought about it for all the time we were on the rafts; I especially brooded on what the Captain had said, no more lies. I couldn't stop thinking about it. I eventually realised that was the closest he would ever get to an apology. He wouldn't say he was sorry for his lies. He didn't feel it. But he would say, no more lies. His life of lies on the Wall had used him up. Nothing before the sea was real. Nothing before this, here and now, was real. I could understand why they might say that, if they had reconciled themselves to life out here. To me, it felt the other way around: life before this was real, but the sea was a dream or delirium. An afterlife.

I noticed that the Captain stayed well clear[2] of Kellan and made no attempt to be in charge or to lead. The only adult he regularly spoke to was Hifa, because she was doing most of the work of setting up and checking the nets and lines.

'What do you talk about?' I asked her one night. By tacit[3] agreement, the rest of the community let us use the back of the lifeboat as our place to sleep when it wasn't raining. When it rained they

1 remorse: feeling of being sorry about sth. you did **2** stay clear of sb.: stay away from sb. **3** tacit: implicit needed the cover. So although there was no privacy by day, we were able to be intimate in the evening. That meant that the days had a shape, company and work by light and just the two of us by night.

'Nets. Ropes. Fishing. He knows about it, he used to fish back where he came from.'

I thought about that.

'Does he ever talk about it?'

I felt Hifa shake her head in the dark.

'He never talks about the past, or the Wall, or anything. Just nets and rope and fish.'

We lay there listening to the creaking and slapping of the rafts and the water, the faint high note of the wind which, in the lee of the island, we could hear but not feel. You had to take the good moments where you found them, and since memories were painful, and hopes were elusive[1] and tormenting – what if we could sail to here, what if there were no Wall there, what if what if what if – you tried to make the most of the good moments you could find in the present tense. We had some, there in the back of the lifeboat, floating, amniotic[2], in the fuggy[3] air under the awning. When I fell asleep, I always had the same dream, of fire: of looking at a fire in a grate, or a cooking fire, or a bonfire; watching the flames flicker and change shape and feeling their warmth and their glow and thinking, that was funny, it was such a long time since I saw fire that I'd forgotten what it was like, I really missed fire, I'm so glad it's back in my life, I must never take it for granted again, there's really nothing in the world as lovely as a fire, as giving and generous, as sure to make you feel safe, I'm so glad about the fire. When I woke from that dream there were always a few moments when I felt as if the fire were still real, as if I could still feel its glow, still see the flicker, still feel warm and secure, and those moments were the best times I had on the sea.

1 elusive: disappearing quickly **2** amniotic (fluid): *Fruchtwasser* **3** fuggy: not fresh

21

The prevailing wind towards and around the island was very consistent, and came from the south-west with variations in intensity but not much change in terms of direction. It was this which gave us safety in the lee shore and made it possible for the floating community to exist. That's not to say the wind was always completely identical. From the south-west, broadly speaking, yes, but there were many small shifts of a few degrees here, a few degrees there, like someone changing position in their sleep, and they all had a different effect on the rafts, changing the sway and shift of the planking. Some of the rhythms were gentle and regular and easy to get used to, but some of them were jarring[1] and dissonant, making the rafts buck and move out of sync with each other. The members of the community all seemed to have got used to this a long time ago, but I found there were times when I could hardly stand, let alone move, let alone do anything difficult or fiddlesome[2]. I hadn't ever felt sick on the boat, but there were moments on the rafts when I was queasy; it was the chaotic nature of the motion that did it. Hifa noticed but she could tell that I was trying to keep it to myself and she was sympathetic. She had been seasick on the lifeboat but was fine on the rafts.

I stopped counting the days but I think it was a few weeks after we joined the community that the weather took its first proper turn for the worse. There had been bursts of rain, just enough to give a feel for what the winter might be like, but nothing really bad. The night before the storm was completely still and clear. According to Kellan that was a warning sign of bad weather ahead. In the morning we saw thick banked black clouds at the horizon, moving not in the usual direction, straight towards us from the south-west, where

1 jarring: unharmonious **2** fiddlesome (infml): complicated

we would be protected by the island, but at an angle, directly from the south. That was bad news, because it meant the weather would be coming at us more laterally[1] than it ever had before. We started to prepare by pulling in lines and ropes and nets, fastening down the tops of the water containers so they wouldn't spill or be contaminated by salt spray. People worked quickly and knew what they were doing; this wasn't their first time. The girls went round the rafts picking up any loose objects and putting them away. I went to the far end of the rafts where Kellan was looking at the sky. Above us the clouds were slate grey, then a little further they were dark grey, then black. He saw my expression and put his hand on my arm.

'It'll be fine,' he said. I wanted to believe him but the fact that he'd felt the need to say it meant that I didn't. My worry, the obvious worry, was that the weather's change in direction, combined with the strength of the winds and waves, would be so strong that the rafts were torn from their anchorage and broken apart. Realistically, that was likely to happen one day, so why not today? I stood and watched for a while. The storm came closer and the swell began to move differently. The rafts started to float and dance. The teenagers looked like I felt, apprehensive, but the younger children thought it was fun and funny; they giggled and ran about and flicked bits of water at each other, and ignored the adults who tried to grab them and get them to calm down. They only stopped messing around when the bad weather hit, which it did suddenly and frighteningly. The storm began with a sheet of wind and rain racing sideways at us, visible from at least a kilometre away. The slanted stinging rain drenched us at a forty-five-degree angle, and the ocean hit the rafts with a giant rolling punch from below. The rafts soared and buckled and were pulled apart from each other, but held. I was still standing next to Kellan. He was calm but intent, looking in the direction from where the weather was coming, squinting a little against the rain and wind.

1 laterally: from the side

That first impact made me think we could not survive the storm – that the community would be ripped apart. I walked as fast as I could over the kicking, plunging rafts back to our lifeboat. I climbed aboard and got in under the awning in the back of the boat, where Hifa and Hughes were already sitting. I wondered for a moment where James and the Captain were riding out[1] the storm. I did not think it would sink us, sink the lifeboat, but I did think it would mean we couldn't stay together as a collective; the rafts and boats would be scattered over the seas and we would have to look for each other or for a different place of temporary safety. The sensation of despair, which I had been holding at bay[2] ever since we had been put to sea – I suppose because we had been so busy with the work of survival – came back in full force. I was sure the rafts would be forced apart.

I was wrong. The storm never built from that first great thrash[3]. The wind and rain came again and again, but did not grow in intensity and was never more than a series of frightening but brief squalls[4]. We braced ourselves for the weather to build to a crisis, but it didn't happen. The squalls came at irregular intervals, sometimes no more than two minutes apart, sometimes with lulls of fifteen or twenty minutes, followed by a longer and more violent but still manageable gust. I think the island deflected just enough of the storm's force, changed its nature just enough, to save us. I felt sick but didn't actually throw up and was helped (I'm not proud of this) by the fact that Hifa began to look a little green too.

Three small squalls came together, each a little longer than the last, the waves rocking us so little now that no new water was being splashed in. There was a pause of more than twenty minutes and then the shortest, smallest burst of wind and rain so far. The storm was passing. We had survived. The rafts would not be torn apart. The community would keep going. I could have cried with relief. Hifa was still looking green but I reached out and squeezed her arm

1 ride out sth.: come through a difficult situation **2** hold sth. at bay: keep sth. in check **3** thrash (n): blow, hit **4** squall (n): sudden and violent wind

and got up and left the awning and then left the lifeboat to go and look around.

Kellan was still standing on the side of the rafts closest to the island, closest to the storm. He couldn't have been there the whole time, I thought, that would be superhuman; he must have kept coming in and out as the squalls moved on. Elsewhere on the rafts people were coming out of shelters, stretching, beginning to tidy up and straighten up. In the distance the skies moved from a much lighter grey than before to, at the horizon, a paint-roller swipe of bright blue. He turned to me and smiled.

'Told you,' he said.

'I was worried,' I said.

'Sure,' he said. 'But look.' He held out his hand and pointed at the horizon as if he owned it, still smiling, then slowly swung his extended arm from one side of the horizon to the other, and then kept turning and pointing, a single broad swipe, doing a full 360-degree tour of the sea and sky, as if he were revealing his handiwork, the world he had made. When he got to the seaward side of the boat, in the direction where the storm had gone, his face changed, and because I was looking at him and laughing, it was as if what happened began there, with his expression changing, looking, for the first time since I had known him, not just frightened but more than frightened, aghast[1], blanching[2], horrified. I turned to look too and I saw, coming in our direction into the weather and the wind, battering against the waves, a big ship, heading straight at us. A gust of wind and rain, the final one of that storm, came and went, and I stood there and got soaked while it passed, wishing that when the sky cleared, the impossible boat would have gone and we would laugh about the shared hallucination. My heart was beating so fast that my chest hurt. It was a ghost boat, something from a dream or nightmare, a phantasm of the rain and mist. We were seeing things. But the squall moved past us and when it did the ship was still there, still coming, still pointed towards us like a knife. It had lights on the

1 aghast: filled with horror **2** blanch: become pale

mast and rigging[1]; the same five lights in a triangular pattern that I had seen weeks before, at night on the open sea. This was the same ship.

1 rigging (n): *Takelage*

22

My first thought was: maybe it'll be OK. Maybe they'll just want to join us ... but that didn't make sense. There could be any number of people on a ship that size, and at the fewest there wouldn't be fewer than say fifteen or twenty, and fifteen adults was too many. Maybe they were coming in peace? But there was, even at first sight, a feeling that they weren't coming in peace. If that ship had been a person they would have been staring at us as they approached, bristling[1] with aggression, looking for any excuse to start a fight.

Kellan did not move and did not speak. He just kept looking at the ship. The rest of the community was now seeing what we were seeing. Everybody stopped what they were doing to stare. Even the children stopped what they were doing. There wasn't a face that didn't seem racked[2] with apprehension. I had sometimes imagined that other arrivals might come to the rafts, but had pictured them arriving the same way we came in the lifeboat, desperate and barely surviving and grateful for any respite from the sea. We had been even more grateful when we found we could be useful and had skills and manpower to contribute. I could imagine a repeat of that. I hadn't imagined this, though. What this ship looked like, more than anything else, was a warship.

The Captain came out from one of the shacks in the middle of the raft and took in what was happening. He went to the end of the community closest to the approaching ship. It was now about two kilometres away. Visibility had been poor during the storm. This ship could only have come across us by chance, just as it had only been by chance that our lifeboat had come to that place. Unless they had naval charts[3] and were looking for the island; in which case they

1 bristle with sth.: be full of sth. **2** rack sb. with sth.: make sb. suffer sth., inflict sth. on sb. **3** naval chart: map of the sea might be professionals, might even be Guards. Perhaps they were looking for us? Our case had been debated, somebody in authority had decided we had been treated unfairly, and the Guards had been sent to look for us and bring us home? This wild thought came to me from nowhere and I suddenly felt sick with hope. Guards sent to save us, Guards sent to save us, I told myself, my mouth dry with fear and longing. I wanted to tell Hifa but knew that I couldn't because I was probably wrong and if I was I would have done a bad thing, given her the hope and then given her the despair. So I stood and stared, speechless, with the rest of them, my feelings strobing between fear and hope. We had no way of defending ourselves, there was nothing we could do.

The Captain was the only one of us who seemed to have a plan or any sense of what to do. He moved down the rafts. He was even more heavy-footed and off-balance than I was on the moving surface. He got to the very far end and stood with his hands on his hips. Hifa had come over to me and Kellan and she asked a question with her expression. I had no answer. We waited. The ship came closer, plunging up and down, the spray over its bows grey-green-white as it smacked into the waves. James and Hughes came over to us too and we all stood together. The squall which had hit us a minute or so before now hit the boat and again I had that childish wish that when it cleared, the ship would have vanished. A magic trick, here one second and gone the next. But when the rain and wind passed, there it still was.

'Let's go over to that end,' said Hifa. So that's what we did, picking our way over the rocking rafts, in between members of the community, towards the Captain. I can't explain the instinct to go and stand with him, other than that it had been ingrained[1] on the Wall, the idea that we were Defenders and that's what Defenders do, you stand there and wait to see what comes. The community looked at us as we walked past. They were standing still and staring; nobody else had moved since they saw the ship. We got to the Captain when

1 ingrained: deep-seated, deep-rooted

it was only a couple of hundred metres away. At closer range, it looked smaller: not a huge ocean-going ship but a practical working boat about the size of a fishing trawler[1]. There were men on deck; fifteen or so. There was no flag or insignia[2] or writing or identification of any kind. I felt something inside me curdle[3]. My heart, already racing, sped up and was now beating as fast as I had ever known it. These were not Guards. These were not our people.

The ship slowed as it got closer to us and came to a halt, with engines running to hold it in place, no more than fifty metres away. At that range the deck loomed far above us and I could only see four men standing at the bow. Three of them had rifles slung over their shoulders. Even with the noise of the wind and waves and the engines, they were well within calling distance, but they didn't say anything. The Captain, at the very end of the rafts, spread his arms to their full width. You could see that the gesture meant: we have no weapons. We are at your bidding[4]. He held the pose for all of ten seconds.

One thing you learn in combat is that when people are shot in the head, they are there one moment, and then they cease to exist. They drop in a way that no living thing drops; they fall to earth like inanimate objects, because that is what they now are. The transition from life to death is instantaneous[5]. That is what happened to the Captain. He seemed to fall before the noise of the shot. He had hit the deck of the raft before I understood what had happened. They had killed him just to make a point. Just like that – gone. I heard Hifa make a noise between a gasp and a cry and heard someone else swearing and realised that it was me.

The ship, what we now understood was a pirate ship, manoeuvred until it was sideways on to the rafts. There were the four men at the bow of the ship and about ten or a dozen armed men standing at the side, pointing weapons at us. They lowered their anchor and a

1 fishing trawler: *Fischkutter* **2** insignia: symbol, sign **3** curdle: (here) freeze (out of fear) **4** be at sb.'s bidding: have to obey sb.'s commands **5** instantaneous [ˌɪnstənˈteɪniəs]: happening immediately

ladder and an inflatable boat and eight of them got in it and crossed over to us. Hifa and I bent down to the Captain's body, lying on the floor of the raft in one of the positions that only the dead adopt, his arms bent under him, his legs folded backwards under his hips, his head, what was left of it, bent down over his chest.

I say 'his' – was he a he any more? Probably not. But it is difficult to think of a dead body, a body so recently dead, as an 'it'. For a few seconds I thought of all the things the Captain had been to me, the different selves he had incarnated[1], from my first minutes on the Wall through the weeks of duty to fighting together to his betrayal to the time at sea; and through all of that the side of his life I had never seen and did not know, the place he had come from, his family, his people, his overt[2] treachery and secret loyalty and the terrible consistency of his courage and his betrayal. The bravest man I would ever know, and the most loyal, and the biggest traitor. He had at one point been the person I admired most; he had saved my life; he had done me more harm than anyone else; if he hadn't directly murdered me, he had come very close. For a moment I felt the force of all those things he had been, ebbing out on the floor of a raft on the open sea. And then the pirates arrived. We were still crouched over him when the first of them got onto the raft and came over to us. He pointed his gun, a semi-automatic rifle, at us and wiggled[3] it from side to side. The gesture clearly meant: step away. Hifa and I got up and moved back a couple of paces. The pirate raised his head and two of the other pirates came over. All three of them slung their guns over their shoulders and they stooped[4] and picked up the Captain's body and pushed it over the side of the raft. It floated for five seconds and then slowly sank.

The first pirate pointed his rifle at us again and jabbed it backwards. We turned and saw that all the other members of the community had gathered in the middle section of the rafts, at the demand

1 incarnate sth.: embody sth., take the form of sth. **2** overt: open, not in secret **3** wiggle sth.: move sth. in short quick movements **4** stoop: stand with bent head and shoulders

of the five other pirates who were walking around the rafts, looking into shelters, opening boxes and water catchments. It was clear that they were taking a rough inventory of everything we had. The thing they looked at longest was our water. They took a long hard look at the stores of firewood and the community's fuel tank, opening it, tapping it on the side and listening to the echo. That made sense. Water and fuel, the two most valuable commodities[1] out on the sea. The pirates who were taking the inventory called the first pirate over in a language I did not recognise. He went across to them and they talked and pointed. I could see that our supply of water was big news to them. Three of them tried our drying fish and gulls and passed them back and forwards between them, with commentary.

After they had taken this quick look around four more pirates joined them and they began a more thorough search. Two of them stood guard over us in the middle of the rafts. They held their rifles pointed directly at us. I read their body language to mean that they thought they would find things; and that when that happened, people would often do something stupid. The other pirates went into every shelter, opened every box, searched every crevice[2] and cranny[3]. It took a long time and while they were doing it we had nothing to do but sit on the floor of the rafts. James started to whisper to me, but the nearest pirate hit him on the shoulder with the butt of his rifle, and the meaning was very clear, so after that we sat in silence. Physical discomfort did nothing to alleviate[4] the fear. I found myself trying to work out not what the pirates would do, because that was obvious: they were going to take everything they wanted. The question I was thinking about instead was, what would they leave? What would we have to help us survive?

The more I thought about it, the more obvious the answer became. The pirates would leave us with nothing. Why would they do anything else? They were people who killed on sight, just to make

1 commodity: thing that is of value because it can be used and/or traded
2 crevice: small opening **3** cranny: small hole **4** alleviate sth.: reduce sth., make sth. more bearable

a point. The benefit to them of leaving us with enough water and food to sustain ourselves was exactly zero. As I was thinking that, two of them came past, carrying the two remaining boxes of supplies from our lifeboat. There was a dummy compartment in the boat with other boxes hidden behind it, which we had tacitly agreed not to tell the community about, not yet anyway. It was our insurance policy and also our guilty little secret. I had been starting to feel ashamed about that, but now it seemed an astute[1] thing to have done. It could be the only food we had left. Enough for what remained of the community for two or three days. Longer, on starvation rations. A week, say. So, not enough. Not by any standards.

I watched the pirates work, systematically stripping the rafts of everything they could carry. There would be rustling and a stifled[2] cry, not from the pirates but from the community, when they came across something precious among people's personal possessions – a jewelled flask, an empty silver picture frame, a ceremonial dagger. When people murmured or cried out, the guards raised their rifles and the community went quiet again. Once the pirates had taken the valuables, they took the food. All of it. They stacked the drying fish and birds onto two racks and four of them carried them over to their boat and then winched[3] them up the side. There was a moment when I thought it was all going to tip over and be lost and I felt panic at the thought and then realised that was stupid because as far as we were concerned it was all lost anyway. After they had taken the food they took the water. There was enough of it that they called for help, and some of their crewmates who had been standing watching from the bow of their ship came over and joined them in the hard work of stealing our water. That went on for a long time: the catchments were heavy. The pirates cursed and sweated as they carried them across the raft and winched them onto their ship. Dark was beginning to fall by the time they had finished.

1 astute: smart **2** stifle sth. [ˈstaɪfl]: restrain sth. **3** winch sth. up: *etw. mit einer Winde noch oben befördern*

When they had taken everything, the pirates came back, this time towards the community where we sat in the middle of the rafts, ten pirates this time, their guns raised, and they barged[1] their way in among us and grabbed the three teenage girls. It happened fast and because it was hard to believe or understand it was also hard to react in time. Hughes, who was standing next to the tallest and oldest of them, stepped in front of them as they dragged her away, and was smashed to the ground by a pirate behind him. He hit Hughes on the back of his head with the stock of his gun. I think Hughes was unconscious before he hit the floor of the rafts. As the pirates pulled the girls away from the group Kellan and Mara ran after them and took hold of the girls, both of them shouting, 'No, no,' and the pirate nearest them stepped backwards and swung the rifle to the left, hitting Kellan in the head, and then to the right, hitting Mara too. Both of them fell to their knees. It took a second at most. The pirate then raised his gun and pointed at the rest of us, as if asking, who's next? No one was next.

They dragged the girls to the far end of the rafts, where their inflatable boat was waiting to take them the fifty or so metres to their ship. All three of the girls were screaming and fighting. The pirates who had been on the rafts started to get on the inflatable, pulling the girls with them; once again, it was so full it looked as if it might tip over. There was a lot of noise from the pirate ship, raised voices, voices in a new tone. I think they were celebrating; some of the voices from the ship sounded drunk, or on the way to drunk.

'No no no no no,' said Hifa. I looked at her and realised something: they would have taken her if they had realised she was a woman. But just like the first time I'd seen her, she was wrapped in multiple thick layers of clothing and had her cap pulled down and you could hardly see her face. They hadn't seen her for who she was. Nausea, and I'm ashamed to say relief, hit me. I can't remember what I said, but James stepped forwards, his hand inside his clothing, and for the first time during the attack, I remembered his grenade.

1 barge: move forward by pushing people out of the way

'I have to stop them,' he said.

I could think of nothing that would stop the pirates except setting off the grenade, which would kill them and anyone near them, including the girls. Then I saw that was what he meant. I could tell Hifa had the same train of thought. We stood looking at each other. Kellan and Mara were hopping and skipping over the rafts towards the pirates, moving, as always, as if they had been born on the water. I remember that clearly: how elegant, even dainty[1], they were as they danced quickly over the rafts that last time. I remember how at ease they were here in their home on the water. They were calling out 'stop' and 'wait' and 'please'. Their voices were frantic, beseeching[2]. The first pirate onto our boat, who had dragged one of the girls away himself, was standing next to the inflatable, still holding her by the arm. He now turned and looked at us. For a second I thought, wait, he's changing his mind. He handed the girl to another pirate, passed her over like a parcel, and then he took his gun down off his shoulder and pointed it at Kellan and Mara, who were running towards him and the inflatable and the ship.

Kellan and Mara did not stop shouting and did not stop running and got to the last section of raft, the one closest to the pirates. Just as they set foot on it, the pirate shot them, Kellan first, then Mara, in the chest. It wasn't like the Captain; they didn't die instantly. Instead they fell and were lying twitching and thrashing and bleeding and coughing blood on the floor of the raft. Several of the pirates laughed and one of them did a little mime[3] of how they had flailed and fallen. The shooter laughed at that, then he braced the rifle against his shoulder and took careful aim and shot them in the head, first Mara, then Kellan. He turned with the gun still at his shoulder and looked over at the rest of us, sitting in the middle of the rafts. Again the look spoke: it was saying, any more? Nobody moved. The pirates got into

1 dainty: graceful **2** beseeching (adj): pleading, imploring **3** mime (n): imitation

the inflatable and crossed to their ship and half carried, half forced the girls up the ladder. There was more cheering and whooping[1].

'I have to,' said James. I think, looking back, he was wanting us to say something or do something that would either change his mind or give him a different idea. I didn't know what to say. I was thinking: Hughes might know what to say or do. The Captain might know. Kellan or Mara might know. But Hughes was unconscious and the others were dead, and I didn't know what to do. James reached inside his clothes and wriggled around under them and took out the grenade. I realised that the explosion would be unpredictable and dangerous for the rafts so I began moving people down towards the back of the community and told them to get into shelter where they could find it, and keep their heads down. I went over to Hughes. He was out cold but breathing regularly; the cut on his head was bleeding but it would clot[2] and he was probably going to be OK. He was too heavy to drag away and in any case there was some cover from a nearby shelter so I put him in the recovery position[3] and left him there. I would have covered him with a space blanket if the pirates hadn't taken them all.

James walked slowly across to the pirate ship. There was a gap between our rafts and their vessel. They had taken the inflatable back but their ladder was still down. There was nobody standing guard or looking over at us. The pirates had clearly decided we were no threat to them. He lowered his legs over the side of the raft, then got into the water, holding the grenade in his left arm, above the water. He side-stroked over to the ship, got his right arm on the ladder and stayed there for a few moments. He was gathering his strength or making sure he was certain, or both. Then he started to climb.

Everyone in the community who could move had gone to shelter. Five people apart from the two of us. Before the pirates came we

1 whoop: make a loud sound out of happiness or excitement **2** clot (v): *gerinnen*
3 recovery position: *stabile Seitenlage*

had been fifteen strong. Most of them didn't know exactly what was happening but they had done what Hifa and I told them to do.

'We need to get to cover,' I said to her. She nodded and we both crossed to our lifeboat. A gust of wind came and the rafts rocked and we stumbled into each other. That was how we got into the lifeboat, holding onto each other. We sat on the floor of the boat, the back of our heads against the side. For the first time since the pirates had come I was conscious of the movement of the sea, still unquiet after the storm.

'How long?' she said.

'Not long. He'll run towards them. The fuse time is five seconds, yes? He'll probably climb up then prime[1] it, pull the pin, then run at them. They'll kill him as soon as they can but they probably aren't carrying their guns any more, so ...'

'The girls might be at the other end of the ship. We'll have a chance to rescue them. We wait for the bang then we go and see.'

'Yes,' I said, knowing that was unlikely, and that even if we could make it work, the surviving pirates would kill us. But with James having done what he was about to do, we would have to do our part as well. Our odds were so bad without food and water that almost nothing we could do would make them worse. I started counting to ten, then realised there was no point, that it would happen when it happened. The silence – I mean apart from the noise of the wind and water and the creaking rafts – went on for longer than I had thought possible. Maybe James had given up and was coming back towards us. I felt a cowardly twinge[2] of relief at the idea. That was when there was an explosion, a reverberating concussive pulse through the air. I felt my breath catch and could see the same look on Hifa's face. A few seconds later, there was another, much bigger explosion. This was truly huge, a physical sensation more than a noise. It couldn't be the grenade, it was a far bigger bang. I felt the whole structure of the community give a violent jolt, an energy that went through all the rafts and hit our lifeboat in the side. I started to put my head up

1 prime (a bomb): *(eine Bombe) scharf machen* **2** twinge: sudden emotion

but Hifa grabbed me and I knew she was in the right: if we'd had our heads above deck when the second bang happened we could easily have been killed. There could be more to come. I kept my head down and waited. I could hear things, but I wasn't sure what: noises which were neither human nor aquatic[1], not the wind, not the sea. Tearing noises and hissing noises. I waited and waited and eventually said, 'Yes?' Hifa nodded. We both put our heads over the side of the lifeboat.

The rafts had broken up and were on fire. Acrid[2] smoke was pouring up from the tar-soaked ropes that had bound the community together. The pirate ship was on fire too, what was left of it, but the top half of the ship had disappeared. The grenade must have ignited[3] a big supply of either fuel or ammunition or both. The first explosion was the grenade, the second was whatever the first one had set off. There could be no survivors on the ship and not many on the rafts either and the fire was coming towards our lifeboat. The section of raft nearest us had detached from the rest of the community. We were already five or ten metres away from the other rafts, which had broken into three big pieces. 'Our' raft, the one we were tied to, was on fire. The fire was getting closer. I could see no survivors on the other boats, but it was getting dark and in the fire and smoke I might not have been able to see them even if they had been there.

I thought: Hughes. He would still be unconscious, still lying in the recovery position. If the fire hadn't got to him yet. But there was nothing I could do – no way to help my shift twin. The rafts were already torn apart. If I tried to swim to them I would never make it back. There was no choice.

'We have to cut loose,' I said to Hifa, 'or we'll burn.' She looked around and I could see her running the same calculations that I had. Then she nodded and began untying the set of ropes at the stern[4] of the boat while I went to the bow and did the same. The toxic smoke

1 aquatic (adj): relating to water **2** acrid: having a strong unpleasant smell
3 ignite sth.: set sth on fire **4** stern (n): *Heck*

stank and stung. We worked as fast as we could but the soaked, cold, thickly interwoven ropes were almost impossible to untie. It occurred to me that Kellan had tied them like that on purpose, to stop us making a secret getaway. As we struggled with the ropes we drifted further away from the flaming rafts, which we could now see only through the light of their own fire. I realised that the other rafts were anchored, whereas we weren't. We would drift away and there was nothing I could do to stop it. I tried harder to undo the knots but my fingers were tired and numb and shaking with cold. I could see that Hifa was doing no better. The fire on our raft was coming closer and within minutes was going to be at our boat.

Finally, with the bitter, reeking smoke from the fire stinging our eyes and choking our lungs, I worked my rope down to its last threads and was able to tear them apart. I threw the far end of the rope away and went to Hifa and helped her do the same thing. By now we were both frantic. We were starting to feel gusts of heat from the flames and the smoke was suffocating. We picked and tore the rope and, coughing and gasping, threw it over the side. I pushed at the side of the burning, sinking raft to get it away from us. Our lifeboat swung in the current as we moved away from it. The fire and smoke had blocked our view and I now looked for the other rafts. We might have turned around as we floated free, so they could now be behind us; I scanned the sea in all directions, then turned and did it again. I grew more desperate as I realised I couldn't see them. We had drifted too far away. Night had fallen and we were alone on the sea.

23

That night we did nothing except hold each other and let the boat drift. Both of us had inhaled smoke and we both had racking coughs. We were too tired and distraught even to feel frightened. The Captain and Kellan and Mara all dead, James and the girls blown to pieces, the rafts broken up and on fire, the burning hulk[1] of what was left of the pirate ship – they cycled through my mind, one image after the other. I kept thinking about Hughes and how we had left him unconscious. I slept for a little, woke to replay the previous day, then slept again.

When I woke it was just starting to be light and Hifa was still sleeping. I had realised, during the hours of darkness, that there would be one moment to hope for, one moment of possible salvation, and it would come when the sun rose and we could look for the island. There was no way of knowing how far and fast we were drifting. We might be hardly moving. We might be moving at a walking pace, say three miles an hour, so that by daylight we could be more than twenty miles away. I just couldn't tell. If we could see the island, we could row towards it and find what was left of the community. I didn't think that everyone could have survived, but half of them might still be alive, and half of the rafts still workable, and with that we could try to start again. On this lifeboat we had some food and water, but the community, what was left of it, had none. Unless we weren't the only ones with a secret cache[2] that the pirates hadn't found. But where we had once built up reserves of food and water, with luck we could do it again. Maybe. We'd just have to get through the first few days with the supplies we had on the lifeboat and hope we were lucky with fresh rainwater.

1 hulk: main part of a ship **2** cache: hidden store

A sign that day had fully broken was when a bar of light came over the side of the lifeboat and illuminated the edge of the awning. I lay where I was for a few minutes, putting off the moment when I would, one way or another, know.

Hifa turned over in semi-sleep. That meant she would be waking up soon. For reasons I can't explain, I wanted to face the facts of our situation for a little while on my own: I wanted to know first. I carefully got up and crawled out from beneath the awning. The day was calm and clear. I took a long slow scan of the horizon, then another, then a third one to be sure. There was a patch of cloud on one point of the horizon that could, just possibly, have been a bank of weather gathering over the island where we had sheltered. I stood and watched it for a few minutes, then looked away, and looked back, and there was no mistaking that the clouds were changing shape and dissipating[1]. They had not gathered over the island. There was nothing else to be seen, at any point of the compass. We had drifted away from the island and the community and were now on the open sea.

A few minutes later, Hifa joined me. By that point we had spent so much time together on the Wall and on the water that the first seven-eighths of any conversation were had in silence. She did the same tour of the horizon I had done, then looked at me. I nodded to say, yes, you're right, I've looked too and there's nothing there.

'I'll set up the water catchments and the lines, you do the inventory. Or the other way around,' said Hifa. I could see in her face the same thoughts I'd been having, not of fear – there would be time for that later – but sadness and loss. The people who weren't with us any more were still there in her eyes. No doubt she could see the same thing in me.

'Inventory,' I said.

So that's what I did. The secret compartment was under a false panel at the back of the boat. Even though I knew it was there, it still took me a moment to find, and I had a wild second of panic

1 dissipate: disappear slowly

when I thought I'd been imagining the hidden cache – but no, it was just a very clever design, a fake plank fitting seamlessly with the real planks around it. Thank God, because otherwise the pirates would have found it, and we would have been as good as dead already. I opened the compartment and started sorting through what we had. The news was good. My rough calculation was four weeks' food, more if we were very careful and didn't do too much manual work. There was only about a week's water, but my hunch was that with only two of us, given how much rain there was, we could probably make it to four weeks with water too. Lack of food kills you in three weeks, lack of water in three days. We would be OK for a little while.

No sooner had Hifa finished putting out the lines than she was pulling two of them in again, mackerel wriggling on the end. I tried to take that as a good omen. She killed them and put the lines back out again. Then she wiped her hands on herself and came and sat next to me where I was putting the food stores back in the hidden compartment.

'Plan?' she said.

I shook my head. I said: 'We're drifting south-west, I think. Away from the Wall. But I'm guessing. I don't really know where we are.'

'The Captain's plan was to head south. He said there were places where people would help us.'

'He said he knew places – we don't. Big difference.'

Hifa shrugged. I shrugged too. I can't remember who spoke first and who agreed, but what we settled on was, south. Towards the places where the Others came from. It made sense: we were Others now.

For the next week we did a mixture of drifting and gentle rowing to correct our course. We had no compass so the navigation wasn't rough and ready so much as rough and rougher. There were sharp ups and downs to our emotions, not just hour by hour but minute by minute. There were times when I could imagine finding settle-able land, finding food, finding somewhere we could live peaceably for the rest of our lives, be happy, even live a kind of idyll, and other times when I came close to thinking the best thing would be just to get over the side of the lifeboat and swim away from it until my strength gave out and the end came. Hifa at times was affectionate, at times irritable, at times silent, and there were even times when we joked and laughed as much as when we were back in our private room in barracks on the Wall. We cuddled to keep warm and even had sex once or twice. Death and sex – close companions. We didn't talk much about what had happened, and when we did, we were quick to absolve[1] ourselves. There wasn't much that we could have done that was any different, or would have made any difference. There were a lot of ways we could have got ourselves killed too.

We caught a few fish. We collected some rainwater. I think those supplies extended our probable survival time by about a week to ten days. I told Hifa I was trying not to think about it, but in truth I was running calculations all the time: how long we had left, how far we could drift or row, what were our odds. I thought we would be unlucky to head roughly south for a month and not come across land at any point, but I also had no illusions about just how unlucky it was possible to be. As Sarge would have pointed out, if we weren't freakishly unlucky, we wouldn't be here in the first place.

On the afternoon of the eighth day, I saw something on the horizon. I went through that usual sea-sequence of thinking something is a cloud, then suspecting/hoping it might not be, then the hope growing, then ecstatically letting yourself accept that hope is justified. The thing I could see was too square, too abrupt in its angles, to be a natural object. We were past caution, so we adjusted our direction and started rowing towards it, hard shifts of thirty minutes each. We were desperate to get there while it was light, because we knew that once darkness had fallen we might never find it again, whatever it was. We could drift away from it in the night as we had drifted away from the island. So it was now or never. My hands had grown unused to rowing when we were on the rafts, but the diving had helped me to get reasonably fit, and having a destination in sight made it easier too. We rowed for about three hours. As we

1 absolve sb. (from sth.): decide not to blame sb. (for sth.)

came closer it became apparent that it was an oil or gas installation. From a distance there was no way of telling if it was inhabited or not. At closer and closer range, that was still true. There was nobody to be seen on deck and no sign of activity.

'What if we can't get up it?' Hifa asked, while I was rowing. She was standing at the front of the boat, not looking at me but at the platform. She had read my mind, because once I realised what the platform was, I had begun to worry that there would be no means of getting off the lifeboat and onto the structure; that we would bump up against it as we almost had against the island, and find no way of climbing aboard. The disappointment of that could kill me.

'It's some sort of installation, there must be ways on and off it,' I said, sounding, to my own ears anyway, a lot more confident than I felt. The platform was close now, so I rowed and kept rowing, but the currents here were adverse, and it was harder work than I had thought possible to close the last few hundred metres. At this range you couldn't see how it worked. It was an oil or gas rig[1]; I couldn't tell, and wouldn't have known how to tell, the difference. The main deck was high, seventy metres or so above the water. There was a tower on the main deck. The whole structure was supported on four legs, which as we got closer could be seen to each have one thick main pillar and another smaller one attached to it.

Since the attack on the Wall, I had learnt to expect the worst. That was proving to be a useful habit. We came to the structure and manoeuvred alongside the nearest leg so that the currents would press us against it and it would take less work at the oars to hold us in place. There was no ladder there, but I didn't panic. There were four main legs, each with an inner leg, so there were eight places where we might find a ladder. Eight chances. One down, seven to go. Hifa held the lifeboat in place with small movements of the oars, while I took a break to recover some strength. My arms were shaking and weak from the rowing. Once we moved from that spot, we would need enough muscular strength to row back to the structure

1 rig (n): *Bohrinsel*

against the currents. I took fifteen minutes to rest, then braced myself for the next thing. I guessed that we had half an hour of light left at the most and I had by now convinced myself that this was our last chance; if we didn't find a ladder now it would be too dark and we would be too weak, and we wouldn't be able to hold ourselves in place all night. We pushed off and I rowed while Hifa looked. It didn't take long to check the inside legs. Then we took a turn around the outside, fighting hard not to drift too far from the platform and then fighting harder to row back to it.

No luck. There was no ladder, no handhold, no dangling ropes, nothing. No hope. Hifa didn't say anything and nor did I. I rowed back to our starting position, panting, my arms burning, the taste of blood in the back of my throat. At that point, it might have made as much sense to let the current pull us away from the platform, to give up on the hope of it and let it go, but the sea was so big and we were so alone that it was impossible to leave a site where people had been, where human activity had made its mark, even if it offered nothing for us. The light was starting to fade now. I thought we might have enough rope to loop around one of the inner legs of the platform and tie us in place until the morning. Then we could decide what to do next.

'Hang on a minute,' said Hifa. She pointed across the platform to one of the inner legs on the far side. 'I don't remember that being there ten minutes ago.'

I looked. I blinked, rubbed my eyes, and looked again. A ladder was clearly visible. For a moment I doubted what I was seeing, then realised that it must be a retractable[1] ladder and that somebody had extended it for us. That meant two things, two very important things, two things so important and so wonderful that I could hardly believe them: that we were not alone, and that somebody was making us welcome.

I was suddenly feeling a lot less tired. I pushed off and rowed across underneath the platform and we tied ourselves up to the lad-

1 retractable: designed for being pulled back in

der and then looked at each other to see who should go up first. Hifa nodded and took off her cap and shook out her hair, and set off. There was a small stage halfway up and I let her get to it before following her. I'm not great with heights and that thirty-five metres of ladder felt like a hell of a lot of ladder. My arms were jelly when I got to her.

'I don't know what to wish for,' she said.

'I know. Best just to wait and see.'

Hifa set off up the next stretch of ladder. This went all the way to the main deck. She passed through a circular hole at the top and I started up after her. I should have been boiling with thoughts about what was up there and what would happen next, but all I could think about was how I hated being so high up with nothing but a ladder to cling to. I told myself not to look down, but told myself so insistently that it turned into a mantra[1], (don't) look down look down look down. I got to the top and pulled myself through and lay on the metal main deck, trembling all over and gasping for breath. I don't think I could have pulled myself up a single further rung of the ladder. But I didn't have to. We had made it.

1 mantra: word or phrase that is repeated again and again, e.g. when praying

24

We were in a small alcove or entrance hallway at the top of the ladder. Hifa was sitting ten feet away, cross-legged, waiting for me. One third of the platform was open to the elements. At the edge, you could look down and see the sea. From where I collapsed on the floor, all I could see was cloud and the gathering dark. The other two thirds of the platform were taken up by the tower, with this alcove[1] as the only entrance. The sides of the walls facing us were lined with sheet metal. The only way through the alcove into the tower was via a metal door.

When I got my breath back, I said, 'No reception committee?'

She shook her head. 'Just me. But we can't go further. We're locked out.' I walked over to the door and tried the handle. It didn't move. I tried to rattle the frame, but it stayed as still as concrete. The door wasn't just locked but bolted[2]. It had the solidity of an industrial piece of architecture; not the kind of door you can kick in, and from the outside, there was no lock to pick. There was no way through unless someone allowed us through. But it wasn't all bad news. On the floor of the platform, next to the immovable door, were a plastic jug of water and a small paper bag. I opened the bag and did a double take[3] at the contents: six power bars of the kind we had been given when we were on the Wall. I looked at Hifa, and she shrugged back at me.

'Somebody making us welcome,' she said. 'Or sort-of-welcome. We're being watched.'

'You'd have thought so. Not sure who by, though.'

'So now what?'

'Let's just sit here for a bit.'

1 alcove: *Nische* **2** bolted: *verriegelt* **3** do a double take at sth.: look twice at sth. because it is so surprising

So we did. It wasn't as if we had much choice, that evening, after the day we had had. We sat on the platform and waited to get our strength back. The sun was right on the horizon now and the sky had cleared for dusk. The grey metal platform was flooded by incongruously beautiful evening light. It was good to feel that this night at least we would be dry and safe. When I stopped shaking, Hifa and I ate the power bars, slowly and deliberately. The very first bite was of dried red fruits, the same as the first one I had had on my first morning on the Wall. It gave me an overwhelming flashback: I was suddenly back there between Hifa and Shoona, aching with longing for the twelve hours to go past. It felt as if that was ten minutes ago; it felt as if that was two lifetimes ago.

When we had finished the power bars, it was dark. In the alcove next to the locked door, we were sheltered from the wind, and it wasn't cold. We lay back against the corner of the metal walls. Hifa snuggled against me and we settled down for the night.

'This is weird,' she said.

'Yes,' I said, and I was so tired I could hear myself slurring.[1] 'But good weird. Tomorrow we'll find out.' I didn't say what we'd find out, because I didn't know. But I felt sure we'd find something out. I fell asleep with Hifa's head on my shoulder.

The next time I opened my eyes, we were lying the other way around, with my head on her shoulder, and it was bright day. The night had passed in a state more like unconsciousness than sleep. We must have been out cold for at least eight hours. Hifa was still out; I was so stiff I felt as if my bones would crack before my muscles would bend. My neck was cricked[2], my arms were both heavy and stinging, my right leg was cramping and my left leg had gone dead. Despite all that, I felt good. We were up here rather than out there. My intuition told me that we were safe; at a minimum, safer than we had been, and maybe much better than that. As slowly as I could, trying not to wake Hifa, I leant over and started to stretch and as I

1 slur (v): pronounce words unclearly because you are tired or drunk **2** cricked (adj): stiffened

did so, turning my head, I saw something which made me feel even better: a fresh jug of water had been left out and, better still, in fact the best news ever, the door that had been bolted shut the night before was now ajar.[1]

I got up and went to the edge of the ladder and looked down. I could see the end of our lifeboat, which meant it was still there tied up; good. For a few minutes I looked around the horizon. It was a clear day with little cloud and not much wind, and I could see a very long way; blue sky and blue-green sea and not a sign of boats or planes anywhere. Good. I shook Hifa awake, gently at first, and then more firmly.

She blinked, opened her eyes, took a moment to focus. I could see her putting together what had happened, where we were.

'Ouch,' she said. 'Wow. What?'

I pointed at the door. Hifa jumped up, going from groggy and just-woken to fully alert in a split second. Then she exhaled and slowed herself down for a moment, and we looked at each other. And then we went through the alcove door into the tower.

The inside of the tower was, at first sight, hard to take in[2]. The only light came in through slit[3]-like windows high in the walls and, as we entered from the bright outdoors, it was initially difficult to see anything at all. I gradually took in an impression of what seemed to be complete chaos. The floor was covered in pipes and cables and metal boxes and wooden crates, many of them partly smashed. On the side of the room closest to the door, where we were standing, the debris[4] was piled so high it was almost impassable. I didn't trust myself to clamber[5] over the obstacle course until I could see properly, so we stood there for a few minutes and tried to understand what we were seeing. Then we began pushing through the mess. We stepped over and between pipes and cables and metal boxes as we went. This, the ground floor of the installation's tower, had evidently

1 ajar: slightly open **2** take sth. in: take notice of sth. **3** slit (n): long narrow opening **4** debris ['debriː]: pieces of rubbish lying about **5** clamber: climb with a lot of effort

been some kind of control centre. The far side of the room had seven or eight computer monitors, all of them black and silent. There were stacks of computer equipment on the floor of the room's far half. The sense of mess and abandon was absolute.

There was a metal ladder in the corner of the room, the same kind that we'd used to get up onto the platform, passing through a circular hole in the floor above. We slowly and carefully climbed up it, Hifa going first. On this upper floor, the second of the tower's three storeys, the windows were bigger and it was much easier to see. And that is where we met our host. A pale, very thin man, wearing nothing but black drawstring trousers[1], was squatting in the far corner of the room. He was just this side of emaciated[2]; you could see his ribs, which were heaving in and out; he was panting with what must have been excitement or fear. His face was covered in thick dark beard and the only part of it easily visible was his eyes, which were wide and startled. He could have been any age from thirty to sixty. He was sitting next to one of the windows. Beside him, resting with the end down on the floor, was a metre-long telescope. That was clearly how he had spotted us and monitored our approach. In front of him was a cardboard box. The box was resting on a small low table, like a footstool. The bottom of the box had been removed and it had been placed on its side so the cardboard looked like a proscenium arch[3]. On the floor also were small torn fragments of paper, folded over so they could stand up.

'Hello,' said Hifa. She walked across to him and squatted down so that she was at the same level as he was. I followed her and did the same. 'My name is Hifa and this is Kavanagh. Thank you very much for lowering the ladder for us. You saved our lives.'

The man said nothing but moved some of the pieces of paper around while looking at them through the box. My first thought: he's lost his mind, he doesn't know who he is or where he is or what

1 drawstring trousers: trousers that have a cord with which you can tighten them **2** emaciated: thin and weak **3** proscenium arch: frame of a theatre stage

he's doing. But there was something about the game he was playing which seemed orderly and full of intent. The pieces of paper were just that, pieces of paper in different colours, but they had been carefully folded, and he now took all of them out of the box apart from one tall piece and a small flatter piece. He moved them around and then he picked other pieces of paper up and put them in the box and moved them around too. I watched him for a little while but there was no evident pattern to what he was doing. Hifa and I gave each other a quick look.

'Do you mind if we take a little tour?' said Hifa. The man made no reply but his head twitched. It might have been an involuntary movement but we decided to take it as a yes. We straightened up from our squatting and, like the pirates on the floating community, set out to take an inventory. As on the lower floor, the whole of this level was one big room. It was divided into two halves; our new friend was in the tidier section, where there were a number of chairs and a table covered in papers, as well as his cardboard box and telescope.

The other half of the room was as chaotic as it had been downstairs: an obstacle course of boxes and crates and huge circular cans. Hifa and I moved over to check what was in them, giving frequent looks back at the man, who didn't seem at all bothered by what we were doing – he had gone back to shuffling his bits of paper around inside the cardboard box. Some of the crates I recognised as food crates, of the same type that we had on the lifeboat. I tapped the sides of them as I passed; about half were empty, about a quarter were part full, about a quarter were completely full. I felt a surge of hope, of joy. One of the full crates had a partially open lid; I lifted it and looked inside. There was a lot of food here, really a lot. It didn't matter how old the tins inside were, this stuff lasted forever. As for the big storage cans, they might be water or they might be oil, but it was hard to think of anything else they could be, and whether they were water or oil, it was the best imaginable news. Hifa and I looked a question at each other and decided that we would wait a little before we opened them to find out. We didn't want to seem as if we were launching a hostile takeover. We had just got here and who knew what our host might be thinking.

We went up the ladder to the next and last storey of the tower. Here again the windows were even bigger, so there was gradually more light as you went further up inside the tower. It was full morning now and blazingly bright[1]. The layout on this floor was different. These had been, it seemed, the living quarters, divided into rooms off a central corridor, with huge windows at each end, so it was as if you were looking straight out into the sky. It was noticeably warm, not just sunlight-warm but central-heated warm – the first time I had felt external heat since we had been put to sea. I hadn't really expected to feel warm ever again. Hifa and I turned to each other. Her eyes were huge.

We went into the first room. It seemed to be where the tower's sole occupant lived. There was a mattress on the floor and a chair with some bedding folded over it. On the bedding there was a thick paperback book with a torn cover. I picked it up to find the title page. It was the complete works of Shakespeare. When I put it back, the chair moved, and I could see what was sitting on the floor behind it – the best thing of all, the best possible thing, an oil lamp. My heart jumped. But maybe it was a defunct[2] object, part of the detritus[3] and debris that were everywhere in the tower? Surely there couldn't be ... I sniffed: I thought I could smell something I knew well but hadn't come across for what felt like a very long time. I sniffed again: I was sure: oil. I heard a sound which might have been Hifa catching her breath or could easily have been me catching mine.

'Oh my God,' said Hifa. 'Oh my God.'

'However much there is, it's a finite supply, it can't last forever,' I said.

'Yes but it's oil,' said Hifa, which was true. It was oil. I wanted to shout, oil, oil, oil! Light and heat. In that moment I realised some-

1 blazingly bright: extremely bright **2** defunct: no longer operating **3** detritus: remnants of things that are no longer used

thing. I had internalised the idea that I would never again have light and heat – would never have control of them, would never be able to make it bright or make it warm, just by deciding that's what I wanted. An ordinary miracle, a thing we had done dozens, maybe hundreds of times a day all our lives before the sea, and which had then gone away for ever, and had now come back. I felt something strange on my face and touched it and found that I was crying. So was Hifa: not contortedly or in grief, but with tears running openly down her cheeks. I reached out and touched them and she did the same to me.

'I never thought ...' I said.

'Nor did I.'

Hifa couldn't say anything more, she just shook her head in a way that meant yes, oh my God. We checked the other rooms. One was fitted out as a kitchen. The cooker and fridge and other appliances were useless because there was no electricity, but we could see that the man in the tower opened his tins and ate his food here, and cleaned up after himself. There would probably be a way of cooking hot food – where you can make light, you can make heat – but he had chosen not to. The other rooms on the top storey had mattresses on the floor but were otherwise derelict[1]. It was evident that people had lived here. The rooms were big, with space for at least four people; say twelve in total at the platform. They had sailed off, or died in accidents or gone to some other fate. I felt an abstract curiosity and an abstract empathy, and also, at the same time, I didn't really care. Hifa and I were here and they were somewhere else. We decided to take the room with the view towards the west, to avoid being woken early by the sun. We shifted mattresses around, got a table and chairs, and giddily[2], unbelievingly, set up our bedroom as if we were children playing House.

1 derelict: not used, deserted, neglected **2** giddy: excited and happy

25

Hifa and I simultaneously realised that we were starving. We helped ourselves to two of the tins that were sitting in the kitchen – one of beef stew, one of chicken curry. These were flavours we had got very used to in our time on the Wall. Cold, and straight out of the tin, they tasted better than they ever had. We swapped tins halfway though. Hifa had eaten slightly more than her share of the curry, but I forgave her.

'What do you think his deal is?' I said to Hifa. 'Whoever was here went away or died but he stayed because why – he thought it was safer? He wanted to look after the installation, or thought it was his responsibility? Or he just wanted to hide from the world?'

She played with a spoon in the bottom of her empty tin.

'My guess is the last one. Maybe he's just a hermit[1]. Who took pity on us.'

'Well, here's to the hermit,' I said, raising my tin. 'Our hermit.'

'Our hermit,' said Hifa, clinking her tin against mine.

We went downstairs to the second level of the tower.

'We're going to go and get the stuff from our boat,' Hifa told the hermit. He was still at his box, moving his bits of paper around. 'We have food and supplies. We think they will be safer in the tower. But there's quite a lot of it so it will take a long time. I hope that's OK.'

He gave no sign of having heard.

Hifa and I looked at each other. His lack of response, indeed everything about him, was eerie, but there was nothing we could do to make it less so. He had taken us in; he had opened the door; that was all we could ask for. We went down to the lowest floor of the tower, and then opened the metal door out onto the platform. I looked down at the ladder, and further down at the sea far below,

1 hermit: *Einsiedler*

and felt sick with vertigo[1]. After all we had gone through, all we had seen and done, it felt pathetic that I was still afraid of heights. And yet there was no denying: I was still afraid of heights. The drop to sea level was more than two hundred feet: say, two hundred and thirty feet, the height of a twenty-three-storey building, accessible only by that vertical metal ladder. I knew that the more frightened I was, the more likely I was to panic halfway, to tense up on the ladder and be unable to move. I also knew that there was no alternative, no plan B, nobody to carry me or shove me back up: if I froze, I'd be stuck until and unless I either unfroze or fell. I could feel myself starting to hyperventilate.

I sat down on the platform and took my glasses off and put them in my pocket and tried to slow my breathing. It didn't work, and then after a while it did. Sometimes you can take strength from the thought that you have no choice. I got up and without delaying any further, started down the ladder. I stared straight ahead and counted the rungs in tens and tried to go not too fast and not too slow. Hifa waited at the top, probably because she thought I might freak out and start climbing back up and she didn't want to be in the way. I counted ten rungs, then another ten, and ten more, and lost count of how many sets I had done, and suddenly I was at the halfway resting stage. The sea was much closer from here. I knew I would be able to do it. Hifa came down the ladder much more quickly than I had and gave me a hug.

'It's going to be OK from here,' she said. And it was, at first – though it was very hard physical work, as hard as any I had ever done. We decided to empty the storage compartment of the lifeboat. There was a security-blanket feeling[2] to keeping our secret supplies of food and water, but we couldn't guarantee that somebody wouldn't come and take our boat. If they came to the installation, which somebody at some stage was likely to do, and couldn't get up it, which was also likely – in fact was certain, since we knew from

1 vertigo: uneasy feeling that some people get when they look down from a high place **2** security-blanket feeling to sth.: doing sth. gives you a feeling of security

experience that the only way up was up the ladder, and the only way up the ladder was if the occupants chose to let you use it – then the only thing for them to take would be our lifeboat and its contents.

The decision was simple, but the work of carrying everything up to the platform was not. The tinned food was in boxes and we couldn't think of any way to get those up the ladder. The only possible course of action was to take everything out of the boxes and carry it up in our pockets and in a single small heavy-duty bag which would go over the shoulders and leave our arms free. It would be three trips each to take care of the food, and another five each to move the water. We decided to do it in stages, first carrying our load to the halfway resting point. The formula was, drag self up the ladder, dump what we were hefting[1], collapse onto the platform and wait until our arms had stopped burning, then go back down the ladder, rest again for a few moments, repeat. As the day went on the rests grew gradually longer and less effective. By the time we had each taken eight trips, the halfway platform was full of boxes and cans and bottles and my whole body was burning and shaking.

I was lying on the floor of the halfway platform when Hifa came up, threw the last contents of the lifeboat beside me and dropped to the metal deck, gasping with effort. By now we had each climbed nearly a thousand feet of vertical ladder and the sun was low in the afternoon sky. We must have lain there without speaking for the best part of half an hour. I didn't feel much better for the rest.

'This isn't going to happen,' I said. 'Not today.'

'No,' said Hifa, still lying on her back.

'I don't even know how I'm going to make it up from here.'

'Me neither.'

'Let alone carry everything.'

We lay there for a little while longer. It was oddly peaceful. The resting stage had a low metal ledge around the outside, and when we were lying down, we were below the lip, so we were sheltered from

1 heft sth.: lift or carry sth. heavy

the wind but could still feel the effect of the sun. I felt no impulse to move or be anywhere else.

'We have to go down one more time, to check the ropes. And then we're done,' said Hifa.

'OK. But not today.'

'No, not today.'

She took two power bars out of a trouser pocket and slid one over to me. I unwrapped it and started eating. It was mainly nuts, pleasantly complicated in flavour but very drying in the mouth. I raided[1] the supply of water, took several swigs, then passed the flagon[2] to Hifa. She had already finished her bar.

'We leave all this stuff here tonight,' she said. 'Tomorrow we finish. Then we can retract the ladder, and we're safe.'

'Safe.' I could feel myself tearing up[3] at the word, my eyes swimming; a sign of how exhausted I was. Safe. We lay there on the platform, barely moving or speaking, for a long time. The sun had lost its warmth, and was starting to head for the horizon, when Hifa sat up and said that it was time for us to get going.

'We don't want to be on the ladder in the dark,' she said. 'We don't want the hermit to forget that we're here.'

I was a little groggy and stiff and still felt weak from the earlier exertions. That's why I made my mistake. I said, 'Fine. You go first.' She nodded, stretched, bent to give me a kiss on the cheek, and started up the ladder. I gradually stood, rolled my neck, looked around the empty horizon, yawned and looked up. Hifa had gone; she had climbed the ladder in record time and was nowhere to be seen.

'Hello?' I yelled up. She either was in the alcove at the top of the ladder and couldn't hear me, or had gone inside.

I put my hands on the ladder and started up. At first I felt all right but quickly, within a few sets of ten rungs, realised I was in trouble. It didn't feel like fear, not at first, just that my body would not do what

1 raid sth.: plunder sth., go through sth. and take everything you need **2** flagon: container for drinks **3** tear up: start crying

my mind told it to. I was too weak. I could plant my feet on the rungs well enough, but the strength in my hands and arms simply wasn't there. It was a little like the old days on the Wall, of type 1 and type 2 cold. This was type 2 fatigue. It wasn't going to get better after a few minutes' rest. It was getting worse, and I was getting weaker, and the ladder was seeming longer and steeper with every second I spent on it. I looked up and the platform was as distant as the sky. Hifa wasn't there. I took the risk of looking down. That too was far, much too far to drop. If I tried to slip down the ladder and recover on the platform I would certainly fall. I was trapped.

On the Wall, the closest thing you ever got to loneliness was when you were standing at your post for a twelve-hour shift; but even then you could see the other Defenders, you could hear chatter on your communicator. On the sea I had never been on my own. I hadn't spent a second entirely on my own for months. Now I felt completely alone and abandoned as I never had before. It was me and this ladder, alone in the universe. I was hyperventilating and failing[1] fast. I realised, after everything I had gone through, that I could die here. I could slip and fall and be gone.

I pulled myself up one rung. It was the thought of dying which made me do it – my revulsion[2] at the idea of dying here and now, after everything. Then one more rung. Then another. Not here, not now, I thought. I stopped counting in tens. I just allowed the sense of wrongness and injustice to drive me. Wrong, no, can't die here, one rung. Unfair, unlucky, unjust, wrong, another step. No hope, no future, no chance, no luck, wrong, unfair. That's how I drove myself upwards, after I had nothing else left.

I was at the platform. I pushed through the hole at the top of the ladder and lay on the metal floor. I was so weak and gasping so hard I didn't even feel relief. I had never been so spent[3]. I felt sick, then knew I was going to be sick, then was. I don't know how long I lay

1 fail (v): (here) become weaker **2** revulsion: aversion, disgust **3** spent (adj): exhausted

there, half conscious. I felt movement and Hifa was standing there beside the doorway.

'I don't know how I made it,' she said. 'I threw up.'

I nodded. I couldn't speak yet. She handed me a water bottle and sat down next to me. I swallowed a few mouthfuls, and immediately felt sweat blossom on my forehead. I was so exhausted that even drinking water made me feel a little out of breath. We sat there for a while longer. The sun was going down and the light was beginning to fade; it was around the same time of day we had arrived at the platform twenty-four hours ago.

'We're going to sleep on a mattress tonight,' I said. Hifa's face lit up.

'I know,' she said. 'Let's go in. If you're ready.'

I made a gesture which meant, I'm ready to try. She unfolded herself to her feet and held out a hand. I waved it away and tried to get directly up but wasn't strong enough. I reached for her hand again and with Hifa's help was able to get to my feet. My legs were sore but functioning. It was the upper half of my body which felt useless.

'I thought I wasn't going to make it,' I said. I'm not sure if it was clear whether I meant up the ladder or up onto my feet, but Hifa nodded as if she understood. She held the door open for me and we went through into the chaotic lower level of the tower. We picked our way through the debris. I shook my head at the wall of blank monitors, the control centre for activities which would never happen here again.

Another ladder, up to the hermit's level. This one felt very different from the long ladder down to the sea. Hifa went up first and I followed. This room too was the same as it had been in the morning, the hermit in the same place, on the far side of the room, with his pieces of paper and his cardboard box. It seemed perfectly possible that he hadn't moved all day. One difference was that this time he looked up as we came in, not a flinching or covert[1] glance but a definite sustained look, then went back to his compulsive game. I

1 covert: hidden, secret

walked across the room and stood over him for a moment. He didn't look up and he kept shuffling his bits of paper around.

'Thank you again,' said Hifa. 'We would have been lost without you.'

'Why?' I asked. 'Why did you let us on?' He looked up at me. I felt he was really seeing me, connecting with the reality of my presence in front of him, for the first time. Maybe he saw my exhaustion, and maybe also he saw in my face the trace of what I had been through that day, how close I had come to being defeated by the climb up the ladder. He very deliberately reached out and picked up all the pieces of paper on the floor of the cardboard box. He put them down next to him. Then he picked one of them back up, looked at it, looked at me and Hifa, and replaced the folded piece of paper in the middle of the box. He looked at us again. Then he put all the other pieces of paper back in the box, left them there for a moment, and removed them all so that the same piece, the first one, was the only one left. I suddenly saw what this was, what the box meant: he had created a version of theatre or television for himself and he moved the pieces around to tell stories. He was putting on a show. So what did this mean?

He went through the same sequence again: leaving the central piece in place, he filled the floor of the box, then emptied it. He looked through the cardboard box at the central piece in the middle of the table – in the centre of the stage, occupying the whole of the screen, in his mind. Then, slowly and deliberately, he looked up at me and Hifa.

'He's lonely,' I said. And then to the man: 'There used to be people here, but they all went away, and now you're on your own, and you got tired of it.'

I saw something flare[1] in his eyes: the first moment I'd really felt contact with what was in the mind of our hermit.

'That must have been hard,' said Hifa. He looked at her: yes. His expression did not change. He brought some more pieces of paper

1 flare: *flackern*

to the box and moved them around and watched them. Now that I knew he was trying to tell a story his actions made much more sense. I felt as if I understood: the pieces of paper were other people, other sea-going vessels, coming to the platform. He moved them in circles around the central piece, one by one, and then put them to one side. The central piece, the one representing our hermit himself, stayed where it was. Other boats had come to the platform but he had not lowered the ladder. He repeated this sequence six or seven times. I could tell they were separate actions because he didn't reuse the pieces but put them to one side once he had finished with them. At one stage three different pieces of paper were brought to the platform and he moved them round it in circles, then put them down, then moved them around again.

Three ships had come to the platform and had stayed there for several days, looking for a way onto it. That must have been terrifying. If they had got onto the installation and found him and realised that he had been refusing to let them on, they would have killed him. I wondered if they had guessed that he was there, observing them? Like when you hide from a knock on the door, hoping that the person outside will go away, but then they ring the bell, and knock louder and louder, again and again, knocking and ringing together, and you know that they know that you're there hiding, and they're getting angrier and angrier, but you're committed to hiding now so there's nothing you can do except duck down, low and quiet, and wait and flinch and hide and long for them to stop and go away, except a secret part of you fears that they never ever will, that they can wait longer than you, outlast you, that it's a contest to the death ... and then they go away and you find you've been holding your breath and it's all fine and you're safe. For now.

He stopped moving the pieces around and took the three ships away. The single piece – the hermit himself – was still in the middle of the box. Then he brought another piece of paper to the edge of the box and left it there for a few seconds. He moved it very slightly and left it again. And again. He kept doing this. I got it: a vessel approaching the installation, but slowly, very slowly. It took at least a couple of minutes for the boat to get to the platform. The boat was moving so slowly that it had to be under sail or oar – and that's when it came to me: this must be the story of how he had seen us coming and what he had decided to do. This was us rowing towards the platform.

Our boat got to the middle of the box, right next to the hermit. He left it there and folded his arms. He had seen us coming, he had seen us arrive, and then he had thought about what to do next. He looked at the pieces on the board, then picked them up and put them down beside the box, and then he looked at us, as if to say: and now here we are.

'Why us?' Hifa asked, her voice soft.

He seemed not to be listening, but after a few seconds, he held up two fingers. The answer appeared to be, because there were only two of us.

'Thank you,' said Hifa. The man gave a circular movement of his head which I took to mean something along the lines of 'Don't mention it'.

'Thank you,' I said. It was nowhere near a large enough statement for what I felt, but what else was there to say?

'We're going to go upstairs,' I said. 'I hope that's OK.' Again he showed no reaction, but there was something about his non-reaction which was a form of 'yes'. Yes-stillness was different from no-stillness. This was going to take some getting used to as a form of communication, learning a new non-language.

I went up the ladder first this time. There was just enough light. I went first to 'our' room to check that it was all as we had left it. Hifa came in behind me and sat on one of the mattresses. I knew that I should eat but I felt too tired. I knew what I wanted instead: light. I went to see if there was another one of those oil lanterns. There didn't seem to be one in any of the other rooms on this floor, except the hermit's, and I couldn't take that. By now the sun had gone down. The ladder was the darkest point of the building, in the centre away from the windows, and I went down very carefully. The hermit was still in the same corner, but looking out the windows in the direction where the sun had set. Past him I could see the first stars.

'I'm on the hunt for one of those lanterns,' I said, 'with your permission. It's been such a long time.'

There was a pause of a few seconds. I think it was still so strange to him hearing human speech again that it was taking him a while to process what he heard. He pointed at a far corner of the room. That was a huge moment, the first gesture he had made that didn't involve his cardboard stage set. I picked my way through the stacked and teetering[1] supplies and found, sitting on top of a crate, an oil lantern, identical to the one I had seen upstairs in his room. Next to it, just as miraculous, was a box of matches. It occurred to me that the matches were as valuable as the oil. I turned to look at him and, with the starlight behind him and the moonlight pouring across the windows in front, he made a double-handed gesture which clearly meant: go, take it.

I went back up to Hifa. She was still sitting on the mattress. I showed her my bounty[2], my booty[3], my plunder, my gift. She scooched[4] over on the mattress and I sat next to her. My hand shaking – I was nervous, now that it had dawned on me how precious the matches were – I opened the window of the lantern, turned the tiny tap for the oil supply, and struck a match. Its flare of light was the most extraordinary thing I had seen in a long time. I touched it to the wick[5] and the lantern came into life. The light was yellow-blue, gold, the most beautiful thing I had ever seen. I bent forwards and put the lantern down on a chair at the end of the bed. The light was flickering but reliable, the most cinematic and biggest sight. I sat down next to Hifa and we watched the light for many minutes.

'We can bring the supplies up tomorrow,' I eventually said.

'I'll set out lines.'

'He'll withdraw the ladder. Maybe he already has.'

1 teetering: (here) appearing to be about to fall over **2** bounty: reward
3 booty: valuable things stolen by soldiers in times of war **4** scooch over: move over **5** wick: *Docht*

'But we'll leave the lifeboat there. You never know.'

'You never know.'

We were silent again for a long while.

'I didn't actually want to Breed,' said Hifa. 'It was more about wanting sex. And wanting to get off the Wall. I got tired of waiting, I thought you'd never ask.'

Did I believe her? I'm not sure. Jokes ran through my mind: I thought about saying, I know, or You did the right thing, or Now she tells me. Instead I just squeezed her arm. I thought, I could watch this light forever, I will never tire of watching this light, this light is the best thing I have ever seen. My arms and back hurt, I was tired and hungry, I was, when I thought about it, dehydrated, with a dry mouth and a nasty headache, but I didn't care about any of that, all I wanted to do was sit on the bed and watch the lantern.

'Tell me a story,' said Hifa.

I tried to think of one. 'Everything is going to be all right,' I said, that's what a story is, something where everything turns out all right, but I said that and I could see it wasn't what she wanted to hear. That is another thing a story is, something somebody wants to hear, but my mind was blank and all I could think was, she wants me to tell her a story, a story where something turns out all right. I said this to myself over and over again, that's what a story is, something that turns out all right, and then it came to me, and what I said out loud began like this: 'It's cold on the Wall.'

ADDITIONAL TEXTS

The Wall by John Lanchester review – 'The Others are coming' *Tom Holland*

From Brexit to migration, this masterly climate change dystopia explores contemporary fears with a blend[1] of realism and metaphor

'It's cold on the Wall.' What kind of story might be signalled by such an opening sentence? An adventure set in Roman Britain, perhaps – something by Rudyard Kipling[2] or Rosemary Sutcliff[3], complete with centurions and mists over northern crags[4]. Or a fable of the sort that Jorge Luis Borges[5] or Italo Calvino[6] might have written: a sombre[7] meditation on the correlation between civilisation and frontier systems, composed in the voice of a Confucian[8] scholar exiled to the steppes, plangent[9] with echoes of Chinese poetry. Most obviously, in 2019 any mention of a chilly wall with a capital W is bound to conjure up images of George RR Martin's[10] Night's Watch[11], standing guard amid the snows of northernmost Westeros. Historical fiction, fable, fantasy: the wall is an image potent[12] enough to serve the needs of an entire range of genres.

John Lanchester, in the first pages of his new novel, makes knowing play with this. It is not immediately clear where his wall is, nor why it should be so cold. A mention of trains and lorries is soon a

1 blend (n): mix **2** Rudyard Kipling (1885–1936): English novelist and poet **3** Rosemary Sutcliff (1920–1992): English author of historical fiction and children's books **4** crag: big rock **5** Jorge Luis Borges (1899–1986): Argentine novelist, often seen as the father of magic realism **6** Italo Calvino (1923–1985): Italian novelist **7** sombre: serious and sad **8** Confucian (adj): referring to the disciples of Chinese philosopher Confucius (551–479 BC) **9** plangent: with a strong and loud tone **10** George Raymond Richard Martin (* 1948): US author of *A Song of Ice and Fire* which was turned into the TV series *Game of Thrones* **11** Night's Watch: military order in *Game of Thrones* whose job it is to guard the wall so that enemies cannot enter **12** potent: strong

signpost that we are not on Hadrian's Wall[1], but beyond that the setting remains opaque. There are Captains, there are Sergeants, there are Corporals. Our narrator, it gradually emerges, is a man called Kavanagh, sent to the Wall for an obligatory two-year term of service. As a Defender, his duty is to stare out to sea, and keep watch for people referred to only as Others. Much hangs on his ability to spot them: for every Other who makes it across the Wall, a Defender will be expelled from the country, put out to sea on a boat. The ominous sense of jeopardy[2] that this establishes hangs like a shadow over the entire book.

[...] [P]erhaps, in the wake of a new year when the home secretary proclaimed a state of crisis after a few Iranians had tried to cross the Channel in dinghies, readers will already have guessed. Kavanagh, Lanchester lets slip, is serving on a stretch of the Wall called 'Ilfracombe 4'. Clearly, he has been posted to Devon. Later, he is transferred to Scotland. The Wall, it turns out, is a great mass of concrete that girds[3] the entire coastline of Great Britain.

This, as the clock ticks busily down to Brexit, might seem a pointed and timely satire. Lanchester, however, is not writing as a satirist; his ambitions are altogether more dystopian. Like *The Time Machine*[4] or *Nineteen Eighty-Four*[5], *The Wall* packs its punch[6] by extrapolating a terrifying future from present trends. As HG Wells did in *The Time Machine*, Lanchester portrays a world divided into two classes of people: those who still enjoy a modicum[7] of civilisation, and those who have been excluded from it. As George Orwell did in *Nineteen Eighty-Four*, he portrays a Britain in which rights and liberties have been sacrificed for reasons that seem all too chillingly plausible. Lanchester's horizons, though, are not merely British. No

1 Hadrian's Wall: fortification in Scotland, built by the Romans in the second century AD **2** jeopardy: risk, danger **3** gird sth.: surround sth. **4** *The Time Machine*: 1895 science fiction novel by Herbert George Wells (1866–1946)
5 *Nineteen Eighty-Four*: 1949 dystopian novel by George Orwell (1903–1950)
6 pack one's punch: hit hard, (here) draw one's strength **7** modicum (fml): small amount

country – not even one immured[1] behind concrete – is an island entire of itself. If *The Wall* is only incidentally[2] a satire on Britain's current political crisis, then that is because, viewed through the prism of Lanchester's dystopian vision, Brexit itself is bound to appear incidental.

Kavanagh, gazing out to sea on the north Devon coast, knows perfectly well why he has to serve his time as a Defender. 'Occasionally there would be some big-picture news about crops failing or countries breaking down or coordination between rich countries, or some other emerging detail of the new world we were occupying since the Change.' What has happened is evident from the besetting cold and the fact that Britain appears to have lost 2,000 miles of its coastline. The ice caps have melted; the Gulf Stream has switched; sitting on sandy beaches has become a thing of the past.

While in Britain much has been preserved from the ruin – there is still public transport, pubs are still open, people still go on holiday to the Lake District – elsewhere the effects of the 'Change' have been more devastating. The whole world is on the move. 'The Others are coming': so a government official, visiting a training camp, warns Kavanagh and his fellow Defenders. 'We have had years of relative peace and calm, but that time is now over. You will be busy.'

The Wall, then – for all its obvious echoes of Donald Trump and his own wall, of Viktor Orbán[3] and his barbed wire fences, of Matteo Salvini[4] and his refusal to allow ships carrying migrants into Italian ports – is ultimately no more focused on immigration than it is on Brexit. Both are cast as symptoms of its ultimate theme: climate change.

As an attempt to dramatise an existential threat that seems impossible for humanity properly to conceptualise, *The Wall* is a signal achievement. Lanchester's talents as a novelist – his judicious blending of realism and metaphor, his remarkable ability to ren-

1 immured (fml): shut away **2** incidentally: *nebenbei* **3** Viktor Orbán (* 1963): prime minister of Hungary since 2010 **4** Matteo Salvini (* 1973): Italian Minister of the Interior from 2018 to 2019

der tedium[1] gripping, and his mastery of narrative tension – have been put to estimable use. The result is a novel that ranks alongside Margaret Atwood's *Oryx and Crake*[2] and the oeuvre of Kim Stanley Robinson[3] as a fictional meditation on what climate change may mean for the planet. Even if its value as a work of prophecy is as yet unknowable, it will certainly provide future generations with a mirror held up to the anxieties and forebodings[4] of the early 21st century.

For all that, though, *The Wall* also bears witness to something else: how difficult it is for even the most talented novelist to imagine the future in an original way. Echoes of other dystopias are everywhere. Humans, although not rendered sterile by the Change, have lost the will to breed: and so, as in Atwood's *The Handmaid's Tale*[5] or PD James's[6] *The Children of Men*[7], are haunted by the dread of a terminal demographic collapse. Equally, those huddled behind their concrete fortifications live in fear of the opposite; anxiety about the teeming fertility of migrants has been a constant in apocalyptic fiction. Long before Jean Raspail wrote *The Camp of the Saints* (1973), a novel about mass immigration to western Europe, Victorian novelists were imagining a time when population growth in Asia and Africa would, as Raspail put it, require Europeans to unleash 'a rain of awful death to every breathing thing, a rain that exterminates the hopeless race'.

The Wall is, of course, no paean[8] to racist or eugenicist[9] fantasies – indeed, it is just the opposite – but it is sobering to reflect that the terms of dystopia should seem barely to have altered in a century and a half. This is not to criticise Lanchester, whose novel is

1 tedium (fml): boredom **2** *Oryx and Crake*: 2002 dystopian novel by Canadian novelist Margaret Atwood (* 1939) **3** Kim Stanley Robinson (* 1952): US author of science fiction **4** foreboding (n): powerful feeling that sth. bad is about to happen **5** *The Handmaid's Tale*: 1985 dystopian novel **6** Phyllis Dorothy James (1920–2014): British author of crime fiction **7** *The Chidren of Men*: 1992 dystopian novel **8** paean (fml): hymn, song of praise **9** eugenicist [juːˈdʒiːnɪst]: referring to eugenics, i.e. the idea that humanity can be 'improved' by selecting who can have children and who cannot

so unsettling precisely because it goes so effectively with the grain of contemporary fears; but it is certainly to regret that our fears should seem so impossible to ease.

Tom Holland, 'The Wall by *John Lanchester review – "The Others are coming"',* The Guardian, *19 January 2019, https://www.theguardian.com/books/2019/jan/19/the-wall-john-lanchester-review (accessed 10 January 2020) – Copyright © Guardian News & Media Ltd 2019*

Fahrenheit 451 *Ray Bradbury*

The Wall *bears resemblance to Ray Bradbury's (1920–2012)* Fahrenheit 451 *(1953), possibly one of the most famous dystopian novels ever. In the following passage, Montag, the hero of* Fahrenheit 451, *has just managed to escape from his former home. After the emotional and physical hardships of his solitary escape through river, night, and wilderness, he finally sees a light.*

Half an hour later, cold, and moving carefully on the tracks, fully aware of his entire body, his face, his mouth, his eyes stuffed with blackness, his ears stuffed with sound, his legs prickled with burrs[1] and nettles[2], he saw the fire ahead.

The fire was gone, then back again, like a winking eye. He stopped, afraid he might blow the fire out with a single breath. But the fire was there and he approached warily, from a long way off. It took the better part of fifteen minutes before he drew very close indeed to it, and then he stood looking at it from cover. That small motion, the white and red color, a strange fire because it meant a different thing to him.

It was not burning, it was warming.

He saw many hands held to its warmth, hands without arms, hidden in darkness. Above the hands, motionless faces that were only moved and tossed and flickered with firelight. He hadn't known fire could look this way. He had never thought in his life that it could give as well as take. Even its smell was different.

How long he stood he did not know, but there was a foolish and yet delicious sense of knowing himself as an animal come from the forest, drawn by the fire. He was a thing of brush[3] and liquid eye, of fur and muzzle[4] and hoof, he was a thing of horn and blood that

1 burr: *Klette* **2** nettle: *Nessel* **3** brush: *Unterholz* **4** muzzle: an animal's mouth

would smell like autumn if you bled it out on the ground. He stood a long long time, listening to the warm crackle of the flames.

There was a silence gathered all about that fire and the silence was in the men's faces, and time was there, time enough to sit by this rusting track under the trees, and look at the world and turn it over with the eyes, as if it were held to the center of the bonfire, a piece of steel these men were all shaping. It was not only the fire that was different. It was the silence. Montag moved toward this special silence that was concerned with all of the world.

And then the voices began and they were talking, and he could hear nothing of what the voices said, but the sound rose and fell quietly and the voices were turning the world over and looking at it; the voices knew the land and the trees and the city which lay down the track by the river. The voices talked of everything, there was nothing they could not talk about, he knew, from the very cadence and motion and continual stir of curiosity and wonder in them.

And then one of the men looked up and saw him, for the first or perhaps the seventh time, and a voice called to Montag:

'All right, you can come out now!'

Montag stepped back in the shadows.

'It's all right,' the voice said. 'You're welcome here.'

Montag walked slowly toward the fire and the five old men sitting there dressed in dark blue denim pants and jackets and dark blue shirts. He did not know what to say to them.

'Sit down,' said the man who seemed to be the leader of the small group. 'Have some coffee?'

From: Ray Bradbury, Fahrenheit 451, *Cornelsen Senior English Library, Berlin 2005, 2016, pp. 129–130 – Copyright © 1953 Ray Bradbury*

From the Book of Genesis

In another famous text, the dangers of the sea (and how to survive them) are also important.

VI, 5 And GOD saw that the wickedness of man *was* great in the earth, and *that* every imagination of the thoughts of his heart *was* only evil continually. 6 And it repented[1] the LORD that he had made man on the earth, and it grieved him at his heart. 7 And the LORD said, I will destroy man whom I have created from the face of the earth; both man, and beast[2], and the creeping thing, and the fowls[3] of the air; for it repenteth[4] me that I have made them. 8 But Noah found grace in the eyes of the LORD. [...]

13 And God said unto Noah, The end of all flesh is come before me; for the earth is filled with violence through them; and, behold[5], I will destroy them with the earth. 14 Make thee[6] an ark of gopher[7] wood; rooms shalt thou make in the ark, and shalt pitch it within and without with pitch[8]. [...]

VII, 4 For yet seven days, and I will cause it to rain upon the earth forty days and forty nights; and every living substance that I have made will I destroy from off the face of the earth. 5 And Noah did according unto all that the LORD commanded him. [...]

17 And the flood was forty days upon the earth; and the waters increased, and bare up[9] the ark, and it was lift up above the earth. 18 And the waters prevailed[10], and were increased greatly upon the earth; and the ark went upon the face of the waters. 19 And the waters prevailed exceedingly upon the earth; and all the high hills, that were under the whole heaven, were covered. 20 Fifteen cubits[11] upward did the waters prevail; and the mountains were covered.

1 repent: feel sorry that you did sth. that turned out to be bad **2** beast: animal **3** fowl: bird **4** repenteth: repents **5** behold: look, see **6** make thee: make for yourself **7** gopher wood: strong wood **8** pitch (n, v): *Pech, mit Pech abdichten* **9** bare up: move upwards **10** prevail: remain **11** cubit: ancient unit of length

21 And all flesh died that moved upon the earth, both of fowl, and of cattle, and of beast, and of every creeping thing that creepeth[1] upon the earth, and every man: 22 All in whose nostrils[2] was the breath of life, of all that was in the dry land, died. 23 And every living substance was destroyed which was upon the face of the ground, both man, and cattle, and the creeping things, and the fowl of the heaven; and they were destroyed from the earth: and Noah only remained alive, and they that were with him in the ark. 24 And the waters prevailed upon the earth a hundred and fifty days.

From: 1 Mos 6, 5–8, 13–15; 7, 4–5, 17–24 (King James Bible)*; https://www.die-bibel.de/bibeln/online-bibeln/king-james-version-en/bibeltext/bibel/text/lesen/stelle/1/60001/69999/ (accessed 10 January 2020)*

1 creepeth: creeps **2** nostrils: *Nüstern*

The Author

Diversity is probably the term that describes John Lanchester best. The only child to an Irish mother and a South-African born father, Lanchester, born in Hamburg in 1962, had lived in seven countries by the time he was four. He spent much of his childhood in Hong Kong, then still a British crown colony.

As a writer, Lanchester deals with diverse topics, too. Having graduated from Oxford university with a degree in English, he became a restaurant critic before eventually turning to literary journalism and working for *The London Review of Books*. In his journalistic writing, Lanchester focusses, apart from food and technology, on a great many things, and he is one of the UK's most acclaimed writers on finance.

As an author of fiction, Lanchester has published five novels so far. His debut novel *The Debt to Pleasure* (1996) won prestigious literary awards and was followed by novels focusing on diverse, but Lanchesteresque topics such as food, finance, and Hong Kong (*Mr Phillips*, 2000; *Fragrant Harbour*, 2002). In his fourth novel, *Capital* (2012), global warming becomes an important motif – the novel has been turned into a three-part TV series by the BBC.

The inspiration for his latest piece of fiction, *The Wall* (2019), came from a series of recurring dreams, Lanchester maintains. His main ambition for the book, he once aptly remarked, is that it is wrong.

John Lanchester is married to writer Miranda Carter. They live in London with their two children.